Nobody's
Child

# Nobody's

The stirring true story of an unwanted boy who found hope

# Child

## John Robinson

### with Brenda Sloggett

MONARCH
BOOKS

Mill Hill, London and Grand Rapids, Michigan

Published by Monarch Books in the UK 2003,
Concorde House, Grenville Place, Mill Hill, London NW7 3SA.

Distributed by:
UK: STL, PO Box 300, Kingstown Broadway,
Carlisle, Cumbria CA3 0QS;
USA: Kregel Publications, PO Box 2607,
Grand Rapids, Michigan 49501.

ISBN 1 85424 623 2 (UK)
ISBN 0 8254 6214 2 (USA)

**British Library Cataloguing Data**
A catalogue record for this book is available
from the British Library.

*Front cover: William Bain*

Designed and produced for the publisher by
Gazelle Creative Productions,
Concorde House, Grenville Place, Mill Hill,
London NW7 3SA.

Printed in Great Britain.

# CONTENTS

# FOREWORDS

**I** **well remember the first time** I met John Robinson at Soul Survivor '99. He was keen to talk to me about The Tribe coming to Southampton to work with him. All I could think was that God was saying that this was the man to head up the new bus ministry we were setting up in Manchester. I don't specialise in "words of knowledge", but that afternoon I knew we had our man. Even though it wasn't the best recruitment practice, I offered him the job! Only a few weeks later he was moving the 250 miles up to Manchester with his wife and two lovely daughters. It has proved to be quite literally an inspired choice. There are few people I know who can relate as well to damaged, dysfunctional teenagers as John, and again and again I've seen him introduce them in the most relevant way to a living faith in Christ. I absolutely love the excited messages I regularly get on my mobile phone whenever John has had the privilege of helping to start someone on that wonderful eternal journey.

John's extraordinary story says two things to me. First, this gospel really works! If you don't believe me look at this life and many others who have come to faith through his ministry. And secondly, this gospel needs to be out there on the streets where it works, not hidden away in our churches. I hope more than anything else that this book will convince many people to do just that: get out from under the bowl and let their light shine, because "The darkness simply cannot overcome the light."

Over the last few years of knowing John I have learned to love him greatly and have regularly heard him share parts of the dramatic story that is written here. Every time I'm amazed and feel like shouting at the top of my voice, "Now you try and tell me there isn't a God!"

Only God could take such a broken life and not only put it back together again, but then use it wonderfully to bring healing and wholeness to many others who have had a similarly bad deal out of life.

It's a privilege to know someone like John and an even greater privilege to know his God who loves to take "unschooled, ordinary" men and women and use them to fulfil his amazing eternal purposes.

*Andy Hawthorne*
Director of The Message Trust

**And they say that Christianity is boring!** After reading this book it won't be possible to say this again.

By any standards this is exciting stuff. A lonely adolescent drifts into petty crime and finds himself in the dark underworld of the street where drink, drugs and violence are part of everyday life. Yet running through this fascinating human story is a parallel "God story". A story about how God never gives up on us, however bad or hopeless we might be. A story about how God never stops loving us, longing for us to come to him for hope, help and healing.

Few of us have had experiences like those described in this book. John's life (so helpfully reported by Brenda Sloggett) stands in stark contrast to the lives of most who will read these pages. Nevertheless it is worth remembering that the God who rescued John from these dramatically difficult circumstances is also interested in rescuing those of us who have come from less colourful backgrounds. In fact God thinks the situation of every human being is dark and difficult and that all of us are in need of his rescue plan. The nice, the rich and the "problem free" are just as much sinners as the prisoner, the addict and the alcoholic! In fact, one of the compelling lessons of this book is about the power of God to save us, whatever our background or situation.

But this is not a Hollywood tale with a sentimental message and an unbelievable ending. John still lives with some of the scars of his past life. Some of the issues will only be resolved in heaven. There are still problems to be faced and tensions to be resolved.

The sheer honesty of this book should encourage us. Life presents us with question marks which are never entirely resolved, even by those with a strong Christian faith. Christians are not perfect; neither does God wave a magic wand to bail them out of every problem. However, as this book describes, God is real, powerful and loving. His rescue act is available to all who come to him in faith. He guarantees deliverance from some problems and his special presence in the problems he does not remove. Added to this he provides a guarantee of a future in heaven which will be free from violence, betrayal and pain of every kind.

I thank God that one day I will join the authors in that special place!

*Stephen Gaukroger*

**The first time I ever met John Robinson** was at Alton Towers during a rally called Youth on Fire. It was a Christian event and the place was buzzing with 7,000 kids from all walks of life. I was in one of the outreach tents talking to my wife, Yvonne, when I felt a hand touch my shoulder. I turned around and there stood this guy that looked as if he belonged in a New York gang: his arms were covered in tattoos and he certainly looked out of place at a Christian event. When he told me he was writing a book I wondered who on earth he was.

When I read his book I couldn't put it down. Now I know who John Robinson is: he's truly a man of God, who has been where many Christians don't go. Most of us have lived quite a secure life, but John hasn't. His life was far from secure; he's been to hell and back and God saved him. I think this is a wonderful book. When we feel that we're being persecuted or that life is difficult, just read this book – then we'll see what a difficult life really is.

*Bobby Ball*

# ACKNOWLEDGEMENTS

I would like to thank all the people, only some of whom are mentioned in the book, who have been an inspiration to me, as well as all those who have stood by me through good and bad times.

Thank you to my wife Gillian and daughters Leah and Natalie for loving me and for being the family I'd always hoped for. I love them so much and I'm so proud of them. Thank you to the family which has become my own: to Maggie and Mike, and Andy and Anita, for being the parents I've never had. Thank you to Jacq and Steph for being my much-loved sisters, and my lovely nephews Luke and Samuel and lovely niece Bethany, and my cracking brother-in-law Neil.

Thank you to my work-mates at The Message for the laughter as well as the tears we've shared, and especially to Wayne for his valuable friendship. Richard, Beth, Chloe, Paul and Nikki – I love you!

Thank you to all the young people whose lives I have shared in, I keep all of you close to my heart. Our church family, St. John's Church, are wonderful.

There are several people in particular who made this book come about. Brenda, who encouraged me to get the book done and lovingly harassed me for each chapter – I will always be grateful for her friendship and support. Thanks to Jan for being a fantastic editor. Thanks to Steve Gaukroger, Andy Hawthorne and Bobby Ball for their forewords.

And most of all thanks to Jesus, for giving me life when the world had given up on me.

John Robinson
June 2003

Chapter 1

# NOBODY'S CHILD

I DON'T REMEMBER A LOT about my childhood: my very earliest memories are of living in a children's home, when I was four or five years old. I remember summer days, big sunny rooms with their windows open, and a warm breeze coming in, scented with grass. Outside there was a walled garden with trees and flowers. I felt safe and special: someone held my hand as we walked to church. There were lots of other children there, and people to look after us – some of them were nuns, and I used to think they looked like penguins in their black and white habits. Everyone was kind, and I was happy enough.

At special times like Christmas and birthdays, some of the other children had visitors. Grown-ups came and took them out for the afternoon or even a weekend, but no one ever came for me. I'd hang around in the garden when the staff called for the children who were going out, thinking that I'd be next, but no one ever called my name. I always ended up walking back indoors in tears. Sometimes I wondered why I didn't have a Mum and Dad, but when I asked where my family was, no one seemed to know anything. Then one day a man arrived to see me.

"Hello, John," he said, "I'm your social worker. I'm

here to help you. You have to live here in care because your Mum is poorly and your Dad's away, so there's no one at home to look after you. You've got eleven brothers and sisters, but they're mostly in children's homes around the country – we're not sure where." I thought this was all rather strange, but it was good to know that I had a family somewhere. They were bound to turn up soon and take me home. But time went on, and there was never any news. When I asked, the social worker said he thought my Mum was still ill. He didn't know anything about my Dad or my brothers and sisters.

Over the years the message varied a little, but not much: bit by bit it became more truthful. "You're in care because your Mum's not well and your Dad's in prison." "Your Mum doesn't want you and we don't know where your Dad is now." "It's best if we don't try to contact your brothers and sisters." "We're going to foster you out, and then you'll have foster brothers and sisters."

Thinking about families made me sad; I suppose I felt hurt and rejected. Other children had Mums and Dads: why couldn't I be the same? Why didn't my family want me? What had I done that was so awful? I thought that probably I was very bad. All I wanted was a Mum to love me and cuddle me when I cried, and a Dad to play football with. All through my childhood I used to daydream that one day my Mum and Dad would turn up, hug me and take me home.

I was 32 when I finally obtained my records from Social Services and found out the truth, but by then I'd learned to deal with my loneliness and pain to a certain extent. I'd lived with the misery and confusion of my childhood for a long while, so the stark facts of my early life scarcely came as a shock.

I was born in Yorkshire in 1963: my mother was an alcoholic, and my father was constantly in and out of prison. I was my mother's eighth child, and some of the older children were already in care; by the time I was placed in care at five months old, I was already suffering neglect. My records stated that neither of my parents wanted me: my father was in prison and my mother was living on state benefits. When she went out drinking she left the children locked in the house.

The same records state that I was placed in ten different foster homes over the years, but every placement failed. I don't have clear memories of anything like as many as that – just fragments of recollections of houses and rooms. Only two or three stand out for me. In the first one I must have been about six: I have muddled memories of constant shouting and noise, of being dragged round by my hair, and being terrified of the broom handles they used to hit me. I was frightened and ran away, and after that there was a hazy time when lots of people came and talked to me. In the end they placed me in a new foster home; they said I would benefit from living in a normal loving family.

The "loving family" lived near a park, in a large house with three floors and a large garden. When they took me upstairs we went past some lovely bedrooms with teddies on the beds, but my bed was in the attic. There was a skylight in the roof, but no electric light, so once the sun went down it was dark. The attic was divided into little cubicles with just enough room for a bed in each, and four of us lived there. My best friend was Kenneth: we got on really well together, holding hands when we went to school and playing together in the park.

I thought it was quite normal to come home from school, have some food, and then go straight up to the attic. We weren't supposed to come downstairs again, and the cubicles were partitioned so the four of us couldn't play together. Every afternoon I tried to look out of the skylight to catch a glimpse of the children playing outside: I could hear their voices but I was too small to see out. As evening came I watched the sky turn black, but no one ever came to put me to bed and say goodnight. At school I used to hear other children talking about their Mums and Dads, and I felt that something was missing in my life, but I didn't know what it was. The only fun I had was with Kenneth.

Then one afternoon Kenneth didn't come home. My foster mum came up to the attic, where I was sitting on my bed, and called me out onto the landing.

"John," she said, "Kenneth is dead. He was your brother."

I was stunned. I didn't really know what death meant, but I knew from her voice that it was bad: Kenneth was gone. But he'd been my brother! Why hadn't anyone told me before?

Her voice seemed to come from a long way away. "He went out to play football, and he just fell over backwards. It was a blood clot or a brain haemorrhage, we think." I had no idea what the long words meant; I just knew that I'd had a brother and he'd gone. My dream of having even a tiny part of a family had been snatched away before I even knew it.

For a while after that I felt utterly miserable. I knew I was all alone in the world. My distress manifested itself in the most obvious way, and I started to wet the bed. I was always punished for this: my foster mother would wait until we were all sitting at the breakfast table, and ask, "Who wet the bed?" Embarrassed and ashamed, I would own up, and my food would be taken away and replaced with mustard sandwiches. I tried to eat them but they made me feel sick and retch. Then I was sent up to the attic and told to stay there. I cried to be allowed out to go to the toilet but no one ever came, so I took the plastic soldiers out of an old tin and used it to wee in.

Sometimes they punished me by keeping me in the attic all day when they went to work. Once I found the door unlocked, so, when I got hungry, I crept downstairs to the kitchen and found some dog biscuits. I took them upstairs and ate them: they were quite nice. No one ever noticed I'd stolen them.

I still wasn't tall enough to climb out of the skylight, but I could open it and let the fresh air in. On sunny days when someone was mowing the lawn, I could smell the freshly cut grass. There was a park just beyond our garden fence, and I could hear children's voices as they played by the stream there. I sat on my bed and dreamed of being outside in the sunshine with them, with a fishing net of my own so I could catch tiddlers. I knew it wouldn't ever happen; to my childish imagination, fishing in the stream was what a normal boy would do – but I wasn't a normal boy. Somehow I must be bad.

I went on wetting the bed, and the punishments continued. One day after breakfast my foster mum stripped me naked and put me in the cellar. It was freezing cold and dark, but there was a thin line of light showing under the door. I got as close to that light as possible: it seemed my only refuge. The day seemed endless. When my foster mum came home from work and let me out I smiled at her and ran up to her hoping for a hug, but there was no response. She let me get dressed and go back up to the attic.

No one seemed to have any idea we were being treated like this: the social worker used to visit the home occasionally, but everything was different then. The three of us would be taken downstairs into the nice bedrooms with the teddies on the beds, and she would look in on us and smile happily and pat us on the head. Then my foster mum would ask her if she'd brought the money, and they'd both go downstairs to talk. Left alone in the bedrooms, we had a wonderful time, jumping on the beds and playing with the toys. We didn't have one teddy in our dark little attic and the beds were so hard they weren't worth jumping on. We shouted and laughed at each other: suddenly we were all happy kids having a great time. Then the front door closed and our foster mum came back upstairs.

"Stop all that noise," she shouted. "Get upstairs again – and if you make any noise up there you'll be in big trouble." We cowered and hurried up to our little cubicles in the attic. I couldn't understand why we were never allowed to sleep in those beds, but none of us ever dared to tell the social worker. We were really scared of our foster mum and dad.

One day after I'd been smacked hard for wetting the bed and put in the attic again, I had an idea. I took one of the wheels off my toy tractor and put it on my penis. It worked: when I woke up in the morning I hadn't wet the bed. I went off to school extremely happy, though I was soon in a lot of pain. When I went to the toilet I saw that my whole penis was badly swollen, and another boy fetched a teacher to help me – by now I was feeling very ill. They rushed me into hospital because the urine was backing up into my kidneys, and both Social Services and the police were contacted. I told them what I'd done, and said that I was scared of wetting the bed, but nothing happened. As soon as I was better I was taken back to the same house. I knew I'd be punished for causing all this fuss: this time all my clothes were taken away when I was shut in the attic.

By now I'd grown a bit taller, and I found that at last I was big enough to reach the skylight properly and climb out. I got up onto the roof and sat there, naked. The neighbours saw me, and someone, somewhere, must have finally decided to take action. They took me away from the foster home.

The next place I can remember was called Forestwood Children's Home. I wasn't happy there, either. We had to call the "parents" Aunt and Uncle, and I was scared of them. At the end of the day all of us had to strip and get into a large double bed, boys and girls together. Auntie and Uncle then hit our bottoms with a slipper really hard until we had red welts on our skin. One day I tried to escape by climbing down the drainpipe from the bathroom window, but Auntie saw me, grabbed me and dragged me back inside by my hair. I knew I wanted to run away, but where could I go? The only other home I knew was the house where I lived in the attic. Even though I'd been so miserable there, at least I knew the other children, so I found my way back, went into the kitchen with the others at teatime and ate a piece of cake. My foster mum wasn't pleased to see me, and she called Social Services.

This time they put me in a special home called a Kanner Unit. I suppose they must have thought I had special problems, because they said they wanted to "monitor my behaviour". I thought it was quite pleasant: we could to go outside and play in the fields nearby and enjoy ourselves. We used to have custard for dinner, and sometimes we were allowed to put some of it in the freezer and eat the frozen custard at bedtime for a treat. I hadn't been allowed this much freedom for a long while. Sometimes we were taken to visit an old people's home. They used to do ballroom dancing, which I thought was really weird, but afterwards they sang some old songs which made me cry. I didn't know why: the old people were really nice and welcomed us. Perhaps I wasn't used to people being kind.

Social Services must have been making some inquiries, and after a while they told me I had no relatives who wanted me, and they'd decided to send me to a Dr Barnardo's Home in Tadcaster.

I felt very apprehensive as we drove through Tadcaster on a bright, crisp spring morning. All I knew about Barnardo's was that it was somewhere that took in unwanted children. I looked out of the car window and saw a pleasant small town with nicely kept shops and houses, and as we drove on there were rolling hills and sheep grazing in fields near the road. Then we turned off the main road at a gabled lodge, and drove slowly up the driveway to the house: it was set in lightly wooded grounds, and there were carpets of snowdrops under the trees. It looked like a nice place, and I began to feel more cheerful. A kind-looking lady welcomed me and took me up to a light, airy dormitory. I only had one change of clothing so my little bundle of possessions fitted easily into one drawer of the cupboard by my bed. It was a wonderful place and I settled in very happily. There were about 30 children of different ages there, and I soon got to know them and made friends.

I think I was about nine years old when I went to Barnardo's, and along with the other primary-school-age children I went to school in the next village. There was a farm behind the school where we could sometimes see the sheep being sheared, and ducks swam in the pond. The classes were small, the teachers were friendly, and I felt happy and secure. Perhaps for the first time in my life I began to enjoy myself. I still envied the other children at school who had Mums and Dads of their own, especially one day when we were supposed to be making a family tree. The teacher saw me sitting at my desk, just staring ahead and doing nothing. When she asked me why, I said, "I can't do this. I haven't got a family – not even a Mum or Dad." The children giggled and someone said, "He's a Barnardo's boy."

The other children from the home sometimes had visits from family members, but I only had visits from the social worker. I hated it when the other children went off with relatives, and I can remember standing at the door in tears with one of the staff beside me.

"Why do they get to go home and I don't?" I asked. She took my hand and held it tightly. "You will go home one day, John," she said. "Perhaps when your mother's better."

I know now it was a lie – my mother didn't want me and would never have me at home – but she meant it kindly. Perhaps she thought it was better for me to have some hope. What it meant was that I grew up with a dream that one day I would meet my mother and she would want me. I longed to be part of a loving family. One Christmas one of the house parents took me home with her, because I had nowhere to go. I had a wonderful time, living in an ordinary house with a real family, and they all seemed to like me. I clung to them when it was time to leave, because I really wanted to stay there. I realise now that I was always looking for a substitute family where I could feel normal, and not be called names at school for being a Barnardo's boy.

I didn't like feeling different from other people. Once some of the other children went away to camp, but I wasn't allowed to join them – I think I was still wetting the bed and the staff didn't think I could handle the situation. Even now I can remember the bus full of children all waving goodbye; I was in floods of tears saying "Why can't I go?"

Nevertheless, Barnardo's offered me the best security it could, and love and guidance too. One day when I was playing football with other children in the grounds of the home, I kicked the ball and it hit the larder window with a resounding smash. Glass splinters went everywhere. Then I saw Mrs Lynch come out of a nearby door with Auntie Joyce in tow. Mrs Lynch was the Principal of Barnardo's and Auntie Joyce was the Matron, so I knew I was really in trouble this time. They were both very caring people, but we didn't mess about when they were around. We used to say Auntie Joyce kept her bedroom door well oiled: late in the evening we sometimes sneaked into one another's rooms to play practical jokes, and we would suddenly hear the swish of Auntie Joyce's dressing gown as she crept quietly along the corridor to restore law and order.

On this occasion Mrs Lynch shouted, "Who kicked that ball?" There was complete silence. I plucked up my courage, timidly raised my hand and said, "It was me. I'm really sorry... I didn't mean it. Will I have to go to another foster home now? I don't want to. I don't want to leave here."

She looked at me for a moment and said gently, "No, John, we love you and you'll be here for a long time. You're not going to another home." My heart raced with excitement as I realised I was safe at last, and I wasn't going to be moved on again. Then she added, "I'll talk to you later about that broken pane of glass." Later that day she gave me a little lecture about being more careful, and I took it all in seriously. Afterwards I went on playing happily; I knew I had to respect property and take some responsibility for my conduct, but I also knew I wasn't going to be rejected or sent away.

Mrs Lynch and Auntie Joyce never pretended to be anything other than "Aunties" to us, but they did their best to give us the kindness, love and nurture we would have had in a normal family, and I've always been grateful to them. Barnardo's gave me the best memories I have of my childhood – playing football with Mrs Lynch's dog Hatty, who liked to push the ball with her paws, or going down to the river and diving off the viaduct with Saleem, an Asian boy who was my best friend. There was a football field and a playground behind the home, and swings in the woods where we used to have our own little adventures. Beside the old coach-road was a pond where we could dip for frogspawn in the spring, and I had a secret place there where I used to go if I was upset. At last I was able to play like an ordinary child, having mock fights with the boys and playing kiss-chase with the girls. Once Saleem and I ran away to watch the lorries and diggers building a new dual carriageway – I think we had some idea of being able to help the builders – but we got hungry and agreed to go back home for a Marmite sandwich!

When I was eleven I had to leave the village school for grammar school. I remember sitting in the assembly hall, absolutely terrified, thinking, "This is the big boys' school." I coped quite well for two or three years, until I started to grow up and began to notice girls. Then I realised that the stigma of being a "Barnardo's boy" was still going to be a problem. I bought some perfume from a second-hand shop and gave it to a girl at school, but a bigger boy saw me and punched me and called me names. I knew I wouldn't ever be able to compete. Why would any girl want to go out with me?

I stopped mixing with the other kids and stayed with the other Barnardo's children, and sometimes we played truant from school and went off into the countryside. We liked to play by the river near the home; in summer we swam, and in winter it flooded and the edges froze, so we took sledges and had lots of fun coming down the hill and sliding on the ice. We used to try to get back to the home at the usual time, but we nearly always got found out and reported.

Eventually one of the social workers thought it might be good for me to make contact with my family, and she managed to get hold of some addresses for me. With great effort and care I wrote several letters to my mother, but she never replied. Then they told me they'd arranged for me to meet one of my older brothers. I was so excited, and told everyone at school about it. It was proof that I wasn't alone in the world – I did have a family somewhere. We met in the children's home, but the meeting didn't go very well: he was six years older than me, and we didn't have anything to talk about. Although we were related, we didn't know one another at all. We never met again –

apparently the Barnardo's staff didn't want me to have much contact with him. He'd been in trouble with the police and they thought he might be a bad influence on me. Then I wrote to my sister but she didn't reply either.

I felt there must really be something wrong with me if no one wanted me. The saddest times were Christmas and birthdays, when all the other children had cards and presents. The staff in the home always sent me a card, but I was always desperately hoping that my mother would send me one. The social worker told me my Mum was living with another man now; she had more children by him, but she couldn't look after them and they'd been put in care too. This news left me in total bewilderment. I didn't even know my own Dad, let alone another man. I wondered how she could love a total stranger but not have any love for me.

I got lazy about studying and my schoolwork began to suffer; there didn't seem to be any point in trying to prepare for the future when no one took any interest in me. At school I was known as a cheerful guy who was always seeking attention and wanting to please the crowd, but the humour was a cover-up for my insecurity. I knew my dream of my parents turning up wasn't ever going to materialise. I wondered what would happen to me when I was old enough to leave Barnardo's, but I couldn't think seriously about growing up. I was too afraid.

I stopped playing with the other kids by the river, and started going into the town instead; I made friends with some older lads who gave me cigarettes.

We used to go and chat in a café, and sometimes we hung round the bus station smoking. I got to know the tough lads at school, because being with them made me feel important. I was fed up with being on my own, the Barnardo's boy. I wanted to be part of a group.

Some of us used to go to the Tadcaster breweries after school. We got over a fence at the back and found loads of reject beer cans with dents in them, and we had a great time drinking and generally being rowdy. I think the owners knew what was going on but they didn't do anything to stop it: we weren't stealing thousands of pounds' worth of beer, only the rejects. It was good fun, and we didn't think we were doing anything wrong. As we grew older we got cocky, off-loading a crate here and there. We got caught a few times, and got told off by the brewery and cautioned by the police, but none of it seemed very serious.

One evening we'd lifted some beer and gone into the town and met some girls. Then we went out into the fields nearby, got into a barn, and sat there laughing and drinking. As it got dark we lit a candle and put it on a beam, but while we were messing about the candle got knocked over and fell into a bale of straw. To our horror a fire started and we couldn't put it out: we scrambled out as fast as we could and ran back across the fields to the children's home, covered in straw. The whole barn blazed up – we could see the fire from Barnardo's windows. Then the police arrived, and I was charged with arson and had to go to court. I told everyone it was an accident, but

I was found guilty and sentenced to six weeks in a Detention Centre.

The Detention Centre was horrible: I was only fourteen, and most of the time I was terrified. We were dressed in blue uniforms and locked in assessment rooms. Our duties were to work in the kitchen and clean the toilets, and we kept the floors so clean you could see your face in them. The staff shouted at us all the time and we had to run everywhere. We ate our meals in silence. There were a lot of big bully boys there with shaved heads, and one night someone came into the dormitory and wrapped me up in a blanket and beat me really hard for being the new boy. At first I didn't try to hit back because I was too scared, but as time went on and the beatings continued, I started to fight back. They used to hit us with a big block of soap – it was like being hit with a brick – and although you got very bruised, the blankets softened the blows so there weren't any broken bones. If you shouted, they used to put a sock in your mouth and tie it there. The staff knew this was going on, but they didn't try to stop it. I think the place was easier to run once a pecking order was established among the boys. I was still wetting the bed, and every morning I tried to hide the sheets, but one day an officer saw them and shouted at me. Everybody in the dormitory knew then, and they started to call me names like "pee-bed". I felt so small and ashamed that I hated myself.

Once, when I was ill with a bad eye infection, one of the Barnardo's staff came to see how I was. When I saw her I burst into tears; I was angry with myself for letting them all down. I knew what I'd done was wrong, but at the same time I felt that my punishment was unduly harsh. The others were just as much to blame as I was, and anyway the fire was an accident. I was resentful about being locked up: the work was hard and the night-time beatings were terrifying. Fourteen days before my release date I was moved into a pre-release unit. I lay on my bed counting the bricks in the wall, and thought, "This is so scary. I will never, ever get into trouble again." I tried to think about the future, and plan what I was going to do with my life. I used to think I'd like to join the police, but that would be impossible now that I had a criminal record. The Detention Centre certainly taught me a lesson, but it didn't give me any hope for the future.

When I was released I went home to Barnardo's and back to school. The staff at the home never mentioned the incident and seemed to have forgotten about it, but I imagined that they looked at me differently now: they didn't know if they could trust me. At school everyone had heard that I'd been in the Detention Centre, and no one wanted to know me. My friends avoided me and it seemed as if I'd never get back to normal life again.

When I was 16 I had a visit from yet another social worker. She said I was too old to be looked after by Barnardo's now; I was taking up a place which was needed by another boy. Now I came under the care of the local authority. I was terrified at the thought of leaving Barnardo's – the only real home I'd ever known – and I had nowhere else to go. However, the staff reassured me that they wouldn't turn me out: they would help me find a hostel or a half-way house to live in. I'd done well at school and could have stayed on and taken exams, but I decided to leave. I'd got a criminal record, and it seemed to me that it didn't matter what exams I passed – no one was going to want to give me a job. The way ahead looked terrible and unknown. "I'm on the move again," I thought. "Where shall I go? How am I going to live?" I was 16 years old, but emotionally I was about ten. Even the temporary security of Barnardo's hadn't succeeded in helping me to develop the maturity I needed to start out in life alone.

Chapter 2 # DESTINATION BORSTAL

THE STAFF AT BARNARDO'S kept their word, and didn't turn me away. They let me live in a caravan in the grounds of the home. At first I thought it was great to have some independence, but the truth was that I didn't have a clue about how to live independently: I couldn't boil an egg and I didn't know how to fill in a form. I never cleaned up the caravan, and I stayed in bed a lot. Sometimes I went down the pub – I'd grown into a big lad, and I looked older than my age. I got a job hod-carrying for a local builder, but it wasn't interesting work, and it felt dull and pointless. I was fed up with everything, and I didn't have any ambition or hope for the future. I was lonely, and wished I had someone I could talk to, but I wasn't very good at relationships. Girlfriends never put up with me for long, because I expected too much of them – I always wanted them to be like a mother and sister as well. Actually, I wanted them to be like a brother, too, a mate to mess around with. Years of having nothing and no one who was special to me had made me selfish. I grabbed what I could get, on my own terms. I was fine while we were just "going out" – I liked the idea of having a girlfriend – but I felt threatened by affection or when a relationship started to get serious. As soon as anyone said "I love you", I got frightened, because I was sure that meant things were about to go wrong. I wouldn't let anyone get close to me because I was afraid of the hurt that would inevitably follow when I lost that love.

Eventually I decided I couldn't bear living alone in the caravan any longer, and I ran away to York. I don't know what I intended to do – I was probably trying to run away from myself. It was a long walk, nearly twelve miles, and when I got hungry I picked potatoes out of the fields to eat raw. When I got to York it was evening, and starting to get cold. I was hunting around in some bins – it's amazing what you can find in bins – and I came across some old clothes. I put them on to try and keep warm, even though one of them was a dress! Some people went past and saw me: I must have looked a real sight. They called the police, and just as I was settling down to try to sleep near some toilets, a police car drew up. "Come on, John," they said, "back to Barnardo's." I only wished I could go back – I always thought of it as the one warm, safe place I knew – but I didn't have a home there any longer. I was growing up, but I didn't know how to handle my independence.

I still had some old school friends in Tadcaster, though, and I started staying at their houses and sleeping on the floor. That didn't last long: no one wanted to get involved with my problems. Then someone suggested that I could get a place in a hostel. The one I found was a few miles away – not that far away really, but far enough from my friends and everything I knew. I moved there, but I was lonely, and at first I didn't find it easy make new friends. It wasn't a proper half-way house, and the residents weren't just homeless, like me. They were older lads, and tough. Most of them were on bail and waiting to go to court on charges of grievous bodily harm, assault and robbery. The staff tried to be helpful and keep an eye on me, but most of the time I felt threatened and fearful.

I tried to settle in, but all my security had gone, and I started having nightmares. I dreamt that I was back in the dark attic, but this time there was no way I would ever get out because the door was locked and the skylight had gone. I used to wake up in a cold sweat. I missed the easy friendships of my home at Barnardo's, especially my best friend Saleem. The other boys at school used to bully him a bit because he couldn't read very well, but I stood up for him. Saleem and I sometimes had mega fights, but we were really good friends, and we stuck together, a bit like my brother Kenneth and I had done. Once we went on an Outward Bound Course for three weeks. We loved it: we got up very early and went swimming in an ice-cold pool, then dressed and went rock climbing, abseiling and canoeing. We had to share the chores, cleaning the toilets and making the beds. Sometimes we made our own tea, with sandwiches made with peanut butter, jam and all sorts of weird and wonderful things. It was a fantastic experience: we had to learn to work together as a team and to look after each other. I think it made me grow up, and it helped to give me a bit more maturity and self-confidence. Unfortunately, I still didn't have enough confidence to stand up to some of the bigger lads I was mixing with at the hostel.

I was desperate for friends, and I wanted to fit in. I really wanted to be as hard as they were – I liked going to the pub with them and ordering a pint: it made me feel grown up. For them, offending was a way of life. They'd get talking and someone would say, "Let's nick that Capri from outside the fish and chip shop." And the next thing, they'd done it: someone would run into the shop, grab the car keys from behind the counter, jump in the car and drive it off. One night we had a few drinks and then broke into a factory and stole some videos to sell on. I was late getting back to the hostel and got into trouble, but that didn't stop me. I wasn't going to keep away from my mates, because I didn't have anyone else.

The hostel found me a place on a government scheme where I did a woodwork course, and that could have helped me get a job, but I didn't really want one. My friends didn't have jobs, and I wanted to hang around with them. Anyway, the scheme only paid about £25 a week, and almost all of it had to be handed over to the hostel for my keep. I couldn't see the point of working all week and still ending up with no money, just like the rest of the lads who'd been hanging out together down the town. They were all involved in crime, shoplifting and stealing cars, and I tagged along. It felt like an adventure, and it was exciting. We used to go into Dewsbury and break into places and take money – but only on commercial premises. We never broke into houses, or mugged anyone. We didn't want to hurt anyone personally, but we were all angry at "the system" and this was our way of getting our own back. I went along with it all – I was bitter, too, at a system that allowed me to be homeless and walk the streets, but was willing to spend hundreds of pounds on keeping me in a Detention Centre where I was beaten up all the time.

One evening we passed a pub where we knew the owners were on holiday, so we put a chair through the window and went in. We weren't afraid because we'd all been drinking already. We helped ourselves to bottles of whisky and even took time to empty the fruit machines. We climbed back out of the window and looked up the road, and to our horror there were masses of police cars with flashing lights coming over the hill towards us. It looked like a scene in a film! One of my mates shouted, "Run for it, or we'll be done!" We had cigarettes and bottles of whisky under our jumpers, and our pockets were filled with cash, but we still managed to run off and jump over a wall. There were bushes on the other side, and we hid there and kept quiet. My heart was pounding as I heard the police coming towards us; my foot was sticking out of the bush but I didn't dare to move. Then they went past – how the dogs didn't sniff us out I will never know! Then we heard the police talking as they boarded up the pub, and it was clear that they knew who we were. I was terrified at the thought of another conviction.

Once the police had gone we went to my mate's room and shared out the loot. Now that we'd escaped we were really pleased with ourselves. We still thought we hadn't done any harm to anyone – "The insurance'll pay" we used to say – but deep down I knew I was getting into a crazy way of life. Still, at least I belonged, and I had a gang of mates to look out for me. It wasn't what I wanted, but somehow I just accepted that this was what my life was like. These were my only friends, and if they were in trouble, and living on the wrong side of the law, so was I. There wasn't anywhere else for me to be.

In the end I left the hostel and went to live with some of my mates – they were squatting in an empty flat on a council estate. The best thing about this place was that it was warm: it had underfloor heating, which for some reason was still working. Otherwise it was horrible. The rooms were completely bare, they stank of urine and vomit, and there were old syringes and rubbish everywhere. Still, you could always get to sleep on those cosy floors. Sometimes there were quite a lot of us there, but we just used the place to hang out in: to stash stolen goods, keep a lookout for the police, and sleep – mostly the girls slept in one room and the lads in another.

We never had any money (none of us had jobs and in those days you couldn't sign on for the dole without a proper address) but there was a café up the road where we used to take the stuff we stole. They'd give us free food in exchange for stolen goods. I suppose we managed on one meal a day – and that was when we were doing well. We took the edge off our hunger with cigarettes and drink. We used to get into night clubs free, because we knew the bouncers, and we could always steal money and cigarettes there – and we'd eat people's crisps and finish their drinks when they left their tables to dance or to go to the toilet.

The people in our gang used every kind of drug: heroin, amphetamines, LSD, glue – even the stuff you could buy to get sticking plaster off your skin (you put it on a wristband and sniffed it). I tried LSD once but it gave me terrible nightmares, so I kept off it. I didn't even like cannabis much: it made me feel sick and I didn't like the feeling that I wasn't completely in control of myself. I needed control, because I was always wary and on edge, and you were never sure what was going to happen next.

We always kept a lookout, afraid that the police would break the door down and raid the place for drugs or stolen goods. We always seemed to be running away from places or from the police. It was exciting and exhilarating but scary, too, with gang fights, people carrying knives and getting glassed. I carried a Bowie knife – a dagger with a blade about a foot long – and when I walked into a bar with my gang behind me I felt like something out of *West Side Story*. I knew I'd got a bit of a reputation to live up to. I was living a fast, hard and dangerous life, and sometimes I was sure that I would just die like this – one fight too many, picked with the wrong person, and that would be it.

Even so, deep down I knew I was always pretending to be tougher than I was. If I thought things were too dangerous, I'd back out. And sometimes I'd be in the middle of a fight and I'd start to feel sorry for the other person, if they were getting the worst of it, and hold back. I got lots of tattoos like all the other lads –

it was another way of showing you belonged – but I kept choosing things that were nice designs. "You can't have that one, John," they'd say, "it's a stupid flower! You've got to have a skull!" I worked hard to cover up my soft side. It wasn't the done thing to show consideration for other people, either. I tried to join in with the dirty talk in the pub when a good-looking girl went past. If I kept quiet, they'd say "What's up with you? You gay or something?" I knew I was going against everything I'd been taught at Barnardo's. They'd given me a foundation of love and support, and taught me to respect other people – and here I was swearing and stealing and fighting and worse. But that was just how life was now. I didn't see that I had any choice.

One day I was in the flat when another gang broke in. They grabbed one of the girls and dragged her out, screaming. I was rigid with shock, but it all happened so fast, there wasn't anything I could do. Then one of our lot burst in through the door and said we were all going after them. The girl had been working as a prostitute for the other gang in Birmingham, and they'd come all the way up here to kidnap her and take her back. We all ran outside and went after them together: I wasn't afraid of a fight, and with my mates behind me I was ready for anything.

The only thing I wasn't up for was serious crime. I was sitting in a pub with a mate and he said, "We're going to do a pub tonight. We're going to hide in the toilets and open the safe when everyone's gone home – there's £25,000 there."

"Don't be daft," I said. "They won't have that much money in a pub. And anyway, what if someone hears you?"

He took a white bundle out of his pocket and showed me a gun, wrapped in a hanky.

"Hey, put that away," I said. "I don't want any guns. This is getting crazy, it's out of my league."

I backed out, but the rest of them went ahead and did the job. Of course there was only about £400 in the safe, and that wasn't enough for them to share out between them, so they started knocking on doors and threatening people with the gun and demanding money. A police armed response team were called and they were arrested and jailed for a long time.

It was a typical train of events – I was mixing with a criminal crowd, and they were all in and out of prison all the time. They were violent, too: I lost count of the number of times I was admitted to hospital with cuts that needed stitches, stab wounds or bruising. Every time I tried to leave the gang I got beaten up. Once I was pinned to the ground and stabbed in the stomach. Someone else threatened to put a knife through my tongue. Another time I had a serious slash to my leg, and a passer-by saw me bleeding and called an ambulance. When it came I said "I'm fine, don't bother," because I was really afraid for my life. In hospital, people ask questions, and I knew the gang would kill me if they thought I'd grassed on them. It was a terrible life but I couldn't see any way out: I didn't know anyone else.

Anyway, I was a useless criminal – I was always getting caught. One day two of us had stolen a television, and we were walking along a wall by the canal, carrying it between us. There was a long drop to the ground on one side, and a drop into the water on the other, and we were staggering along clumsily, like something out of a slapstick comedy, wobbling from side to side. Then my mate let go of his end, leaving me holding the whole thing, and I fell backwards into the canal with the television on top of me. As I came up, spluttering, I could see two policemen standing on the bridge, laughing, while my mate ran off.

Eventually the police caught up with me for everything else, and charged me with three burglaries in the area and 20 TiCs (offences to be taken into consideration when sentencing). The magistrates wouldn't let me out on bail while I was waiting for my case to come up, because I didn't have a permanent address, so I spent five weeks in the regional Remand Centre. It was a grim place. I soon learnt some of the prison survival techniques: we used to make pieces of string from our bedding so that when we were locked in we could pass things like shampoo from window to window. There were plenty of drugs available there, and plenty of violence, too – there were regular fights in the corridors with all sorts of weapons. Then there were the suicides. You'd hear the bell go, banging on the door, panic; then hurrying feet and then silence.

One day it all got through to me, too. I was sitting in my cell and thought, "This is all there is to life: running with a gang of people I'm afraid of, or getting locked up in a prison cell. I've got no future and no hope." Nothing had any meaning any more. I had nothing except sentencing to look forward to, and I felt completely adrift with only darkness and loneliness ahead of me. One of my jobs was cleaning the staff areas – I used to collect the old fag ends and re-use the tobacco to make roll-ups. That evening as I was cleaning I picked up one of the aluminium ash trays as well. Back in my cell I worked on the metal, flexing it over and over until it was weak enough to tear into two sharp-edged pieces. Then I slashed both my wrists.

I sat and watched as the blood poured out into my lap, and I didn't feel a thing. I started to get dizzy and black buzzing clouds swam in front of my eyes, but I wasn't afraid – I just wanted to slip into the darkness and not wake up. Then the door opened and I heard screams: my room-mate had come back and seen all the blood. He called an officer and they dragged me off to the medical unit, and the doctor decided to sew up my wrists there, rather than take me to the local hospital. They put me in a straitjacket and transferred me into a solitary cell. Now things were even worse. Every day was the same, locked up all alone with only my thoughts for company, and my movements restricted by the straitjacket. There wasn't much light in the cell; cockroaches ran across the floor; there was a heavy smell of disinfectant and the only sounds were the screams and shouts of other inmates whose nerves were giving way. It was the darkest time of my life, and I felt totally alone.

It was while I was in the Remand Centre that I first began to think about God. I didn't have any concept of a loving God who cared about me; I just thought of God as someone who was "up there" ready to punish me for all my wrongdoing. When I was at Barnardo's they used to take us to church, but I really hated the way the vicar patted us on the head and said, "Good morning, children," and we all had to reply "Good morning, Vicar." He wore a strange big black frock and gave boring sermons; I spent most of the time thinking about what we'd do when we got home, and whether I could dive off the viaduct into the river. Now, shut up in the Remand Centre, I chose to go to church – really just to get out of the cell. I didn't take a lot of interest in religion. I believed in God, but I didn't think he believed in me. At the time my life was in such a mess that I couldn't imagine anything else, and I was sure it wasn't the sort of life God would approve of. I thought I was too far gone for God to be interested in me.

I remembered all the crazy things I'd done, getting into fights and jumping off bridges to escape the police. Once I'd been in an arcade when another gang cornered a young Asian lad and beat him over the head with a crowbar. The next day a man in traditional Sikh dress, turban and all, came over to me in the shopping centre. He reached inside his coat and pulled out a huge knife.

"Was it you and your friends who beat up my brother?"

"No, it wasn't us!" I said desperately.

"My religion says I can kill to take revenge for him," he said. "I'll slice you up or anybody else if I find who did it."

I was petrified and ran away faster than I'd ever run in my life.

When I thought about things like that, my life felt like a jungle – I never knew what was lying in wait for me. It was full of dangers that I couldn't predict or control, and I was afraid all the time. I hated being locked up, but the outside world was even more frightening.

Eventually my case came up – there were lots of charges and it was too serious for the Magistrates' Court, so it went to the Crown Court where the sentences are heavier. I knew you couldn't be tried twice for the same offence, so it was in my best interests to make a clean breast of things to the police now. There were already so many crimes listed on my record that a few more couldn't make it much worse, but if they were all included, "taken into consideration", they couldn't be brought up again in the future. I made a really thorough job of confessing! I told the police about crimes they hadn't even known about, just to be sure I'd got rid of everything! I knew I could be facing a long sentence, and I wanted to get it over with. After being in the Detention Centre when I was fourteen, and the last few weeks in the Remand Centre, I knew that what lay ahead of me wasn't going to be easy.

When I got to court I was terrified. I didn't know what was going to happen to me. I was pretty sure I was going to end up in prison, but a bit of me thought there was a chance I might get off. I had one strong card to play – my unfortunate background. I often told people I was an orphan, because it seemed to get more sympathy than "I grew up in the care of the local authority". I thought I could make a real sob story out of that: poor little orphan me, brought up in children's homes, no proper family. I had a real chip on my shoulder, and a bit of me still thought that everything that had happened to me was unfair. After all, the arson had been an accident, I hadn't meant to set fire to anything, yet I'd been punished really harshly. And I still thought the crimes I'd been committing recently weren't that serious – after all, we didn't really hurt anyone, did, we? The insurance paid. I was full of self-pity, and I hoped I could persuade the judge to feel sorry for me, too.

It didn't work: I was sentenced to 18 months in Borstal. However, it was going to take a while to sort out which Borstal I was going to, so in the meantime they took me off to prison. In fact, they moved me around, and over the next few weeks I spent time in three different prisons. I'd thought the Detention Centre was awful, but I was in for the shock of my life.

In Armley Prison I was put in a special wing with the others who'd been sentenced to Borstal. At first there was a lot of shouting from them – they felt hard done by, too – but being in the big man's prison you soon learnt to keep your head down. The adult prisoners wouldn't put up with us throwing our weight about. There were beatings and abuse, and lots of people couldn't stand it: there were more suicides. There were fights in the exercise yard, and one day some lads broke the legs off a chair and smashed them over a rival's head; prison officers had to come with dogs to break it up. I had a quick temper and I was used to fighting, so I got involved, too. In the end

I got locked up all the time. I used to look out of my window and see the buses bringing visitors for other inmates. I longed for someone to visit me, but no one ever came except my solicitor. I'd been going out with a girl at the time of my arrest, but she lost interest when I was put inside. Anyway, I'd wrecked that relationship, like so many others. I was resigned to being alone. They moved me on to Durham and then to Strangeways Prison before I finally ended up at Borstal in County Durham. It was 1981, and I was still only 18 years old.

# Chapter 3

# TOUGH TIMES

WE TRAVELLED TO Borstal by bus, all of us hand-cuffed in pairs. As we drove through the hills towards Barnard Castle, I thought how bleak and bare the landscape looked. "There'd be no use trying to leg it from here," I thought. "There's not even a house to hide out in." We drove through the village and arrived at a huge complex of buildings set in huge grounds. It looked a bit like a Butlins holiday camp – if it hadn't been for the high walls and barbed wire surrounding it! As we waited for the big gates to swing open I noticed some girls standing by the road, looking at the coach and watching the prison officers. I waved to them with my free hand, but one of the officers came over and hit me hard: I swore at him and he told me to shut up. I realised that no one was going to mess about here; Borstal was going to be serious.

Inside the gates there was a big reception build-ing, with a secure unit over on one side. Behind it there were lots of smaller buildings, like the huts in army barracks. In fact, the whole place was run rather like a big army camp with a very strict regime. You could earn privileges for good behaviour, and the idea was that you could work your way up, out of the secure unit and into the relative freedom of the open bunkhouses. It didn't work out that way for me, though: I was put straight into the secure unit, and though I worked hard and behaved myself, I never got into the open area – I think that after my suicide attempt they thought they'd better keep an eye on me.

That first day we were all taken into a sort of classroom to wait for the officers to come and start the admissions procedure. As soon as we sat down one of the other lads said to me, "What you looking at me like that for?" I was scared but I didn't want to back down, so I said, "I wasn't looking at you. What's your problem?" He flew at me across the table and I hit out at him. The other lads pulled us apart, because they knew they'd all get into trouble, too, if we were caught fighting. We just managed to settle things down before someone came in. It was a good reminder for me that you had to keep your head down. It was just too easy to get into trouble in there: everyone was irritable and edgy all the time, and the wrong word or look could easily start a fight. Right from the beginning I could see what the place was like. Some of the inmates stole anything they could make money on, they hid drugs in their beds and fought vicious battles. You couldn't relax for a minute.

I had to learn to survive in this tough environment. I soon picked up some of the Borstal tricks such as collecting cigarette ends in the officers' mess, removing the tobacco and mixing it with shredded potato peelings. This "tobacco" was sold to new boys in tins and the price went up quicker than it does in the shops! The value of coins was inflated, too, because there was a constant demand for them to use in the pay phone. Twenty pounds in coins was worth £50 in Borstal.

I was assessed and put into a unit on the top floor. On the first day a big, tattoo-covered bully boy came up to me in the shower. He looked at my tattoos and then punched me really hard and growled, "I'm the boss here."

I thought, "I'm in this place for 18 months. I'm not going to be dictated to for all that time," so I hit back. The prison officer in charge knew what was going on, but he didn't intervene. What I didn't know at the time was that this lad was indeed the "Big Daddy" of all the bullies! He said, "Well, at least you've got the guts to fight back. I'll leave you alone."

I was put into a single cell; it had a bed, a sink, a toilet, and a window that looked out over the fields. The lights went out at eight thirty or nine o'clock, and then you were on your own until the next day. The nights felt very long in there. In the morning you cleaned the floor and stood to attention when the officers came round. If your floor was a mess it was recorded and you were put on a charge. Once again I practised all the tricks of how to communicate with other cells while we were locked up, and items like tobacco, sugar and toothpaste were passed from cell to cell via strings on the windows.

During the day we were kept busy. There was a hard regime of fitness training enforced by strict officers, but at least it kept you fit. There were education facilities, too: I asked to learn how to cook, so I was put into a class to do City and Guilds in Catering. What appealed to me about it was that if you were doing a course you could get day release to the local college. I made that my goal, but I never achieved it, because I got into trouble. I needed money for fags, so I stole some sugar from the kitchen, tying the bag carefully on the inside of my leg so the officers wouldn't find it when I was searched. I thought I'd got away with it, but the bag split and I left a long trail of sugar all the way back to my room! They laughed, but they punished me for it all the same. I was put in a punishment block where the mattress was on the floor and you only got one blanket. When a red light came on you had to get up and go to the door and give your name and number. There were no books and absolutely nothing to do. The punishment block didn't even have a toilet in the cell, so I had to use a bucket, and the smell was awful.

I've never been able to forget those prison odours. There was a different smell around the chaplain – he always smelt of drink! He was a cheerful sort of bloke so I went to his services in the chapel – again it was just a way of passing the time in a different environment. The services mostly seemed irrelevant and boring to me, and I didn't take a lot of notice of what went on. One service was different, though. A group of young people came to visit the Borstal, and they came into the chapel and sang to us. The songs weren't boring old hymns; they had jazzy, modern tunes like pop songs, and they were all about Jesus loving you. Just a little glimmer of what they were singing about started to get through to me. There was a Gideon New Testament in my cell, and in the front there was a list of suggested readings for various problems you might be facing. I looked at the list and thought I had just about all the problems, so I thought I'd better look up the verses! Some of it made good sense, and some of it was a kind of comfort to me, but I still didn't have any idea that God could make a difference to your life.

Reading the Bible reminded me of something that happened when I was at Barnardo's – it was one of the few times in my childhood when I thought about God. I was crossing a busy road, and on the grass verge I saw a little dog that had been hit by a lorry. I ran across and knelt down to comfort the poor thing, but it died while I cradled it in my arms. It took a moment before I realised it was dead – it was gone, its life snuffed out, and there was nothing I could do. For some reason I thought of my brother Kenneth, and how he had died and left me alone, and the awful finality of death hit me again. I started to cry, and I couldn't stop. I left the dog's body by the roadside, and I ran away with tears streaming down my face. I wanted to hide somewhere, so I headed off across the fields to the little church we used to go to. It was empty and quiet inside, and I sat down on a pew near the back, buried my face in my hands, and cried. Gradually my sobs subsided and I felt a bit calmer, and I looked up and saw on the wall a picture of Jesus on the cross. I thought to myself, "What did the guy do wrong that he was put on a cross like that?" Something told me that Jesus really was special. I'd been to enough services to know the basic facts of the gospel: Jesus was the Son of God, and yet he was nailed to the cross for us. I didn't know why looking at him made me feel better: the full significance of the gospel message still hadn't really dawned on me. I remember that I felt calmed and reassured by the encounter in the church, but I still didn't understand what it all meant.

All these memories were stirred up by reading the little Gideon Bible, and I started making sure I went to every service in the chapel. I was looking for something, though I wasn't sure what. Groups of people from outside often came to the Borstal to run services and talk about their faith, and I listened to them with admiration. We were a rough lot, and I thought they had guts to come in and talk to us; I could see they really believed what they said. I didn't want to look too interested, though, so I sat with my mates, secretly trying to smoke a fag and grinning at the girls. Sometimes I hung around afterwards in the hope that there might be someone to talk to, but I never plucked up the courage to say anything. I couldn't look a fool in front of my mates.

One day when I was scrubbing the floor of a big hall in my unit, I realised that I had no contact at all with the outside world. I thought, "I never get a visitor. I never even get a letter." The friends I'd made before I came to Borstal were no friends at all; they never contacted me. My girlfriend had written to me a few times, but now she'd gone off with someone else. Then I thought that I might get a letter – and even a visit – if I wrote to someone first, so I wrote to my social worker. I have a photocopy of the letter, date-stamped 4 September 1981.

> Dear Joe
>
> Well I have settled in here and I am ok
>
> I hope you will come and visit me as soon as you can, cos, as you know I don't get any visites And you said you would come.
>
> I have got a lot to say and I now you will have Mr Fisher has not Bothered to write even though I sent a letter thire But I now that now I am in hire hi has forgottin that I was evir thire I know I let Then down and you know I an sorry. But hi could Just send On lettir it would not hurt.
>
> (one line all crossed through)
>
> Sorry about mess but it's nice to get a letter now and then.
>
> I hope you can come soon cos, I am Doing all right I have Just got 1 week nocked off and I hope to get some more
>
> And could i ask if it is all possible to get some New Clothis in cos, my boots are Ripped my Jumper is a mess and my Jacket is all Rippid. I hope that I not asking to much. I would like to leave hire looking more civirlised At least it would help me find a Job I hope you ar coming
>
> Yours hopefully
>
> John Robinson.

Joe did visit me, but he didn't bring me any clothes – he didn't have a budget for that kind of thing. He did have lots of good advice for me, about how to handle myself in Borstal and how to keep out of trouble when I got out, but I don't think I took much of it in. I knew he was just doing his job, and I realised there was no one outside who really cared about me.

There wasn't anyone inside, either. I had associates in Borstal, but you can't call anyone a friend there. Lots of the lads were in for serious crimes – manslaughter, rape, or grievous bodily harm – and if you were wise you just smiled at one another and learnt to keep your head down. I did try to get alongside some of the boys who were being picked on: helping someone else did seem to make me feel better and less depressed. It stopped me from thinking about myself all the time, too. All the same I often felt sorry for myself, and thought it wasn't fair that I was in prison. It was only much later that I realised I really deserved the sentence I got. I'd caused a lot of trouble, one way and another.

As our sentences began to draw to an end we talked a lot about easy ways to get money. Most of it was pretty unlikely: "We know this Post Office where you can get half a million pounds" and "There's money from a robbery hidden in jam jars and buried in the grounds at this address." It was all "Winnie-the-Pooh land". Some of the lads were convinced by it and left with the sole intention of making money quickly and dishonestly. I used to dream of somehow buying myself a high-powered motor bike, and travelling across America. You have to learn ways of surviving in prison, and it kept you going to have dreams, even though there was a lot of rubbish talked. I still had nights when I couldn't sleep and the hours just dragged by. Sometimes I had panic attacks and thought I might die in my cell and never see the outside world again. Or I'd think I'd end up like some of the old lags I'd met in Armley who were never out of prison for long and just kept coming back. I knew that if ever I got into trouble when I left, I'd be sent down for a very long time.

One of the things everyone dreaded was a "gate arrest". That was when you were released from Borstal, and as soon as you stepped over the threshold, the police arrested you for some other crime you'd committed before you went inside. Then you'd find yourself put in a police cell and back inside in no time. This was the reason I'd been so enthusiastic about confessing absolutely everything before I was sentenced, and making sure everything was listed on those TiCs.

Stepping outside the gates for the first time was both exciting and scary. I'd been looking forward to this moment for so long, and the anticipation had been building up over the last few weeks. I had a release grant of about £50, and my few belongings were packed in a brown bag – a bag I realised made me instantly recognisable as someone who'd just got out of Borstal. I took the train back to Dewsbury, to my old friends and my old life, and I made straight for the pub to have my first drink for 18 months. It tasted great, but it felt a bit like going to the pub when I first left Barnardo's: as if I was a little lad trying to act like a man. I really enjoyed sinking that first pint, though; it was like saying I was back in the real world, and I could cope. Then a few of my old mates came in, and the rest of the evening passed in a blur. At Deerbolt they'd arranged a place for me in a supervised hostel, but I didn't go there. I slept in a doorway, instead. In the morning I was so hungry I stole a loaf of bread and a bottle of milk from a milkman when he was delivering further down the road – another petty theft to add to the list.

The problem with being released from Borstal was that there was no support: after all my dreams of freedom and my plans for making a life for myself, the reality was more mundane. Suddenly, after living in an institution where someone told you what to do all the time, and meals appeared on the table three times a day, you found yourself out on the streets with your days totally unstructured, with no money, no food, and no way of getting either. Getting a job wasn't easy: no one would take me on when they knew I was homeless and had been in Borstal. Even if an employer had been willing to take me on, my appearance meant that I couldn't really do a job where you had to face the public. Even McDonald's wouldn't employ counter staff with scars and tattoos like mine. With no income, I couldn't find anywhere to live, so I spent a lot of time on the streets. I scavenged for bits of food and old sandwiches in waste bins; someone told me I could have applied for food vouchers, but I never did. I often slept on hotel roofs, where there were hot-air vents, or in the huge bins in factory yards – some of them were big enough to walk round in! On a cold night, when you're too hungry to get to sleep, even a prison cell starts looking attractive.

Fortunately it was spring, and the weather wasn't too cold; I hung around shopping centres where it was warm during the day. I was always up early in the morning, but I had to keep on the move, in case someone called the police. I was always hiding: skulking in the shadows at night and dodging round a corner if I saw a police car. Some of the lads were already back inside. They'd stolen a car the same day they left, and found themselves back in Borstal after two weeks of freedom. I was on licence for two years and that meant I'd be recalled, too, if I was convicted of a crime. I certainly didn't want that, though I did get a caution for being drunk and disorderly.

Some of my old friends let me sleep on their floors, and soon I was back with them, getting involved in their criminal activities. I acted as lookout for one mate when he broke into a caravan where he knew there was some money, but we only got about £40 from that. Then he said he knew where there was a factory car park full of brand new cars. Stealing one wouldn't do any harm because they didn't belong to anyone yet, and there was always our favourite excuse: the factory could claim on the insurance. We had a few drinks for Dutch courage and then climbed over the fence and broke into the cars. There were heavy steel gates across the entrance, but my mate crashed through them in the first stolen car, and we followed in the others. What we hadn't reckoned on was the fact that the petrol tanks weren't full – there was only five miles' worth of petrol in them! Before long the engines began to splutter and stop, and we had to abandon the cars on the roadside. It was a crazy adventure and it didn't take the police long to trace us and arrest us.

All my good resolutions in Borstal had come to nothing. I thought I'd learned a lesson, but less than a year later here I was back in Armley Prison, remanded in custody in the young offenders' wing. At least I was warm and well-fed, but I couldn't believe I'd been so stupid as to give up my freedom all over again. I had six weeks to wait for my case to come up in the Crown Court, and who knew what sentence I was going to get this time? Then I had a stroke of unbelievable luck. My solicitor went to the judge in chambers, pleading my case and telling him something of my history. He pointed out that I'd been released from Borstal and was homeless and desperate. I was taken back to the court, where the judge granted me a Conditional Discharge: I was released on condition that I went to live at a bail hostel nearby and started actively looking for work.

"I'm going to give you a chance," he said. "If you don't take it, the next time you'll be going to prison for a very long time."

I was so grateful to that judge. At last someone seemed to understand my problems and was willing to give me another chance.

This time there was no question of sloping off to the pub and drinking the release money. I went straight to the hostel and checked in, with £30 in my pocket and my pathetic collection of belongings stuffed in a black bin liner. I really was resolved not to fail, because I knew what lay ahead of me if I had any more brushes with the law.

I was determined to stay out of trouble and get a job, and at least this time I had an address, even if it was well known locally as a bail hostel. I started work packing boxes in a factory, and holding that job down gave me a lot of confidence. I had a pay packet at the end of the week and a structured way of life, with a bed to go home to and regular meals. I moved on to another job, painting and decorating. The firm that employed me helped me to do a City and Guilds qualification, and eventually I was earning enough to pay my way at the hostel. I was standing on my own two feet at last, I had some new skills, and I was feeling quite proud of myself.

Something else gave me hope for the future, too. The warden of the hostel had a daughter called Shelley,* and we got on well together. As far as I was concerned we were just good friends, but she said she loved me. I knew I didn't love her, but I liked having a girlfriend, and it all seemed to be part of getting my life back together. It was good to have someone who cared about me, and I really wanted to hold on to her. She wanted to get married and eventually I agreed. What could be more secure than that? If we got married, I could have my own home and my own family, and I would belong somewhere at last. We found a flat and settled down together, and it seemed almost too good to be true. It was a new beginning for me and I was determined to make a go of it.

---

*Not her real name. I've changed the names of the people in this part of the story so they can't be identified.

Chapter 4

# A BITTER BETRAYAL

BEING MARRIED TO SHELLEY wasn't easy. We lived across the street from the hostel, so her parents kept a sharp eye on me, and her Mum was always coming round. We didn't have much freedom. Still, I did settle down and stopped going to the pub with my mates every night, though I still went out two or three times a week with my friend Jim. Now I was qualified I was getting better pay at my painting job, so we were able to get a mortgage and buy a house. It was only a little two-up, two-down house in a Victorian terrace, but I thought it was a palace. It had been renovated and it only cost £20,000. I was so happy and excited: everything seemed to be going well for me at last.

I found another job that paid even better, working in a factory making bathrooms and sinks; I could work shifts from 10pm until 6am, or 6am until 10pm, and I was bringing home £500–£600 a week. It meant working long hours but it was worth it, and Shelley and I spent time together at weekends. The extra money came in useful, and we were able to buy an old car and the motorbike I'd always dreamed of. I redecorated the house and did the garden. Life was good, and I owed a lot of it to Shelley; I was glad she'd wanted to get married, and I thought that in time I might get to love her. I thought, "This is it, I've made it now!"

I did not get on all that well with my mother-in-law. It had been her decision that we got married in a Registry Office, even though I would rather have got married in church. Eventually she moved in with us. She said it was to help us, but I was earning good money and we didn't need help. Apart from that, I was happy. I got on well with the people I worked with, and most evenings when I got home from work a few friends would drop in. I admired them because they all had good jobs and had done things like going abroad. We'd chat and have a few drinks and they often stayed quite late, even though I had to get up for work when I was on the early shift.

One evening I came home about half past ten and found Jim there – he said he'd called to lend us a video and he was just leaving. Shelley and I had a row about that. We had quite a few rows in those days, but usually we sorted things out between us and made up afterwards. Then one Sunday, out of the blue, she told me I'd changed, and she didn't like the way I was now. I could hardly believe my ears: I knew I'd changed, but surely it was for the better? She said she'd loved me before, when she thought I was "a bit of a rogue", but my new reformed character was just boring, and she didn't love me any more.

I couldn't think how to make her happy. I worked overtime to earn more money so I could buy her presents, but nothing seemed to please her, and things didn't improve. I was worried at the way we were drifting apart. Then one night when I was working the late shift, I realised I'd left my sandwiches at home, so I went back for them. I thought I'd just go upstairs to see if Shelley was asleep yet, so I crept up and found her with Jim. I leapt to the conclusion that she was having an affair with my friend. I was devastated. I walked straight out of the house, trying to get my head round what was happening.

I didn't go back to work. I went and sat on a bench in the park, staring at nothing in the dark. Where did I go wrong? I'd come so far by my own strength of character: I held down a good job, I had a wife and a lovely home, and yet now I knew it was all sham. I had nothing.

Someone came up to me and said, "Are you all right?" but I didn't answer. I felt numb.

I couldn't face going back home, and I couldn't face going to work. I sat in the park all night, and the next day I wandered round the streets in a sort of daze. I couldn't bear the thought of telling anyone what had happened. Days and nights went by in a blur: eventually I plucked up the courage to go into work, but I found I'd been sacked because I hadn't turned up and hadn't given them any explanation. Everything had crumbled around me, and I was back where I'd been a couple of years before, living on the streets, homeless and unemployed. I did bump into a few friends, and sometimes they let me spend the night in their houses, but even indoors I couldn't sleep properly. After a few months I started to feel really ill. I thought it was just misery and exhaustion, but when I went to see my doctor he seemed to think there was something really wrong. He examined me carefully and said, "I think we'd better get you into hospital. We need to investigate this lump." I knew he thought I had testicular cancer, and I was very frightened. I thought of cancer as a killer disease, and I knew that particular sort could kill a young man. I wondered what the future held – that was, if I had any future. Could my luck get any worse?

I went to the hospital and was taken up to the surgical ward. When I looked across at the bed next to me I saw a guy sitting up in bed reading the Bible. We got talking, and he said, "I know you've been through a lot, but God still loves you. You're special to him." I was so angry with him; first I told him he didn't know anything, then I started to get out of bed to punch him, but he sat there so calmly that I held back. I could see he really did believe what he was saying. I called the nurse and said, "Is this some kind of wind-up? Get this guy out of here! How come he's so cheerful?" The nurse calmed me down, and I turned round to the guy and said, "How come God's so good if you're in here? He can't be much good for you." We got talking, and he didn't seem to mind arguing about it. It didn't matter what I said to him, he always had an answer. Some of it I didn't understand, but I never forgot him saying, "Jesus loves you, John, and he understands all your problems." It sounded great, and I would really have liked to believe it, but I couldn't. I thought he was just another religious nutter. His talk touched a nerve: how could he possibly have any idea of what I'd been through? It just made me angry and I still really wanted to hit him.

The doctors did lots of tests, but in the end they

decided I had to have an exploratory operation. I begged them to call Shelley so that I could at least see her, even if it was only to say goodbye. Two days later a kind nurse told me she'd contacted my wife but she had refused to come. She was going to live abroad with Jim. Gradually the real picture became clear: the house was being repossessed by the building society, because I'd lost my job and couldn't pay the mortgage. We'd run up debts and there was no money left in our bank account; now she was starting divorce proceedings. I lay in the hospital bed in a mood of bleak depression, and as I signed the consent form for the operation I hoped I would die. I had no wife now; no home, no future, no hope.

Even if I survived the operation I could only go back to the streets. In my weakened state I didn't have the strength to fight for my marriage or my home, and I felt totally desolate at the thought of facing major surgery without a single friend or relative to care about me. I went over and over things in my mind, endlessly examining what had happened and trying to see what I could have done to cause it. I'd thought I could trust Jim: I'd never had an inkling that his friendship was two-faced. He'd betrayed my trust, and so had Shelley. I knew we were going through a difficult time but I'd been convinced we could resolve our problems. I'd had no idea that she'd fallen in love with him. Where were my friends now? I looked round the ward and saw lots of people who were seriously ill recovering from surgery, but at least they had visitors. Visiting time was a nightmare: I always hoped that someone would turn up, but no one came. I felt totally alone, and so filled with fear that I couldn't think about anything.

On the day of the operation, a nurse came in holding a bowl of water and a safety razor. She smiled brightly at me.

"Time for a shave," she said.

No one had shown any interest in my appearance before, but I thought maybe they liked their patients to look tidy for the surgeon. I went to put some soap on my chin.

"Not your face!" she laughed. "Down below! We need to see what we're doing!" I was horrified – I was as scared of that razor as I'd ever been of any knife! When she came back with a injection to make me relax, I was glad of it; at least the anaesthetic would make me sleep.

When I came round after the operation, the first thing I did was lift the bed covers and pull up the hospital gown. I could see a line of metal staples up my groin, holding the wound closed, but everything else still seemed to be there, thank goodness. I heaved a sigh of relief. Then the surgeon arrived and told me that there was nothing to worry about. He'd found a large pocket of fluid, which had been drained, but there wasn't any cancer. "You're going to be fine," he added. I turned over and faced the wall so no one would see the tears pouring down my face.

When I left hospital I went back to my old life on the streets, sleeping in the places I knew – round the back of factories, where warm air came out of the heating vents, or in empty skips out of the wind. Sometimes I went into public toilets to get warm from the hand-dryers. Those two years of normal life, with a wife and a house of my own, seemed like a dream. I wasn't hanging out with a gang of criminals this time – I was more of a loner now – but life was still dangerous. One night I got talking to another bloke on the street and we ended up having a fight over a cigarette. My leg was slashed and needed stitching, and I had bad bruising all over my face, so I went back to the doctor.

He cleaned up my cuts all right, but he was more concerned about my state of mind. He could see I was badly depressed, and really didn't care much what happened to me any more. He talked to me for a while, and eventually he said he was going to admit me to a psychiatric ward. He said I was heading for a complete breakdown, and clearly thought I might commit suicide. By this stage I had no self-esteem left. I knew nobody gave a toss about me and I was worthless. At least the doctor seemed to care a bit – enough to want to keep me safe. And there was something else, buried deep inside me. Even then, in my despair, I could sense a little ray of optimism that kept me going. I thought to myself, "Life is tough, but it surely can't get worse. I'm a fighter. I'll get well. Eventually I'll come out of this dark tunnel, and things'll get better."

The psychiatric hospital wasn't too bad: I actually began to develop some sense of self-worth. The nurses were really understanding, and I needed that because I was so lonely. They were continually assessing my mental condition, but I knew I wasn't going mad. I'd told them a bit about my past, and the psychiatrist explained that after everything that had happened to me they thought I might break down completely. I looked pretty bad after my latest spell on the streets. I was bruised from the fights I'd been in, and I had a scar across my head where some drug addicts had slashed me when I didn't have any money to give them. The doctor had shaved my head to stitch my scalp, and I guess I must have looked like Frankenstein's monster!

We were a mix of people on this ward: working men, unemployed and professional – policemen, solicitors and doctors. A lot of the patients were there because of drugs, alcohol, relationship problems or bereavement, and in a strange way I fitted in. Everyone was there because they couldn't handle the things that had happened to them, and it didn't matter if they were rich or well educated; we were all washed up together. I was glad the doctors couldn't find much wrong with me, and I made sure I was always cheerful, hiding my misery behind my smiling face. I don't think it fooled them, though.

I had to go and talk to the psychiatrist each day; he asked me lots of questions and I tried to reply with my usual sense of humour.

"What would you do if I was coming down the road in a battleship?" he asked, so I said, "I'd get in my tank and blow you to bits."

"Where would you get your tank from?" he asked.

"Same place as you got your battleship," I replied. Silly questions needed silly answers, I thought, but he was only trying to get me to talk to him. After a lot of these conversations the doctor said I was progressing well but he wouldn't discharge me because I was homeless. Instead, he wanted to put me on some drug trials. I was very wary about this: I'd heard that doctors got paid for trying out drugs. I'd seen some of the patients looking completely spaced-out after taking their pills; one guy used to have about fifteen tablets of assorted colours every six hours, and he ended up walking around like a zombie. Anyway, when I was given my dose I held the pills in my mouth and then went and spat them down the toilet. I thought, "I've got to look out for myself. There's no one else to do it. I'm only a name and number to them." A few weeks later, when I'd spat hundreds of these tablets down the toilet, I started feeling sorry for the rats. They must have been wandering around the sewers in a daze!

The one drug I did take willingly was temazepam: it made me sleep without dreams. I didn't want to dream and I didn't want to lie awake thinking. At night it was too easy to remember the bad things: the places I'd been shut in – the cellar, the dark attic and the prison cell where I had to use a bucket with that terrible smell. Or the drunken fights and the drug addicts who'd pull a knife on you to get money for drugs. Sometimes I'd start wondering why my Mum had had all those children and never looked after them. Didn't she ever think what life would be like for us without a proper family? Then I'd think of Shelley and Jim going behind my back and cheating on me. Shelley didn't want me, either. It was easier not to think; easier to be asleep, and not hear the awful screams from people who had to be put in padded cells. At least with temazepam I could get some sleep. I had to get away from my memories somehow. Perhaps as time went past, things would get easier, and I wouldn't remember things so vividly. Perhaps one day I'd have the strength to face the outside world again, and try to make a new life for myself.

The nurses didn't mind if I went off the ward. Sometimes they asked me to go down the road to buy cigarettes for them, or get a take-away curry. They knew they could trust me to come back because I had a warm bed at the hospital, and nowhere else to go. They suspected that I wasn't taking my tablets, but they didn't do anything about it. Even they thought I was coping well. I kidded them that I was fine and kept making jokes, though inside I still felt as raw as ever. I knew the hospital was giving me a false sense of security, and I needed to face up to getting on with my life again outside. That meant convincing them all that I was well.

They couldn't keep me there for ever, and eventually they discharged me. I felt elated at first: at least I had my freedom again. I thought that perhaps if I went abroad, I'd be able to make a fresh start, but I wasn't exactly very realistic about it. I decided to go to France and join the Foreign Legion. I made my way south to Dover and bought a ticket to Calais. On the ferry I sat at the bar having a few beers and saying to myself, "This is it, this is the life." Of course, I soon found that it wasn't that simple. I hadn't left my baggage of pain and self-pity in England; I'd brought it with me. I felt the old resentment building up as I watched the other passengers – families with children, couples with their arms round each other, dads with their kids on their shoulders – all laughing and enjoying life. As usual, I felt left out and alone. I said to myself, "I'm never going to be normal like that. I'm never going to have a family."

Calais was a disaster. I realised I hadn't thought anything out properly. I had nowhere to stay, no idea how you found the Foreign Legion, and I couldn't speak French. I hung around and kept pretending that I hadn't been there long and that I was waiting for the next ferry, but in the end I admitted to myself that it was all a waste of time. I couldn't magically change my life by going to France. I managed to get on a ferry back to Dover and sat on the dock smoking a fag and sunk in deep gloom. Nothing I did seemed to do me any good – I always ended up back at the bottom of the pile, homeless, destitute, hungry and alone.

The next day I went to the dole office and they gave me an address and a rail pass to a place in Kent. I still didn't have any money, so I went out and looked in some rubbish bins for something to eat. I felt like a scavenging dog. "Surely I can't get any lower than this," I thought. Then I got the train to Sittingbourne and made my way to the address they'd given me. It was on an industrial estate, and it was yet another hostel for the homeless.

My heart sank when I saw it: it looked more like my old Borstal, with big gates and barbed wire round the high walls – though I think this was more to keep the local vandals out than to keep the residents in.

Inside it was dingy and smelly and full of men drinking and smoking. I was asked the usual questions: "How old are you? Are you on drugs? Do you have a drink problem?" One of the staff looked at me closely when I said I wasn't on anything.

"Are you sure you want to stay here?" he asked. "You really don't want to be here if you can help it."

"I'm sure," I replied. "I haven't got anywhere else to go."

He helped me to fill in forms and gave me some clean clothes. I had a bath and used the flea powder they gave me, and explored the place. The dining room smelt of stale food, but it made my mouth water – I hadn't had a proper meal for nearly a week. Then I was taken to a dormitory with no carpet on the floor, and shown to an old metal-framed bed with a stained mattress and a rough green blanket. They warned me that if I didn't stay on my bed someone else would take it. The room stank; other residents came in with cans of beer, drugs and smokes, and I looked round at the dirty wallpaper and the general atmosphere of despair and thought, "Hell must be like this."

The problem was partly that the place was a "resettlement centre" for supposedly recovering drug addicts and alcoholics, not just a hostel for the homeless. Some of the men were in a bad way; lots of them drank meths and several were incontinent and always vomiting. The whole place smelt of cooking, urine, strong disinfectant and tobacco smoke. In a way, I could see why so many of the residents found it hard to give up the habits that were destroying them: it was so tempting to get lost in a haze of drugs and alcohol to escape the horrible reality.

Some of the characters there weren't so bad. Some of them were "men of the road" – walking from town to town, staying in hostels in the winter months and sleeping outside when it was warmer. They had lots of wise advice, and knew all the best hostels everywhere in the country, the best times to go there, and how long it would take to walk. Lots of them drank, too, and their faces were prematurely aged and weather-beaten by drink and the hard life they led.

We had to be out during the day, supposedly trying to get a job. There were factories all around on the industrial estate, and there were jobs going, but as soon as you mentioned where you lived no one wanted to take you on – the hostel had a really bad reputation. Some of us went round the streets and collected old cans, using a magnet to find out if they were aluminium. They were worth money so we collected them in sacks and sold them for about £12 a day. We had a little trick to ensure that we earned £12: if we thought we didn't have enough cans, we filled some of them with earth to make the sack weigh more. It brought in enough money for fags and booze. I didn't drink a lot because I didn't have enough money; you weren't supposed to bring drink into the hostel but everybody smuggled some in every night. Each day I spent picking up fag ends and old cans and I thought, "I'm just a piece of rubbish myself."

One night at the hostel I went down to the TV

room. One guy was injecting booze into his veins and others were melting temazepam capsules and injecting the liquid. There was hardly anyone who was clear-headed enough to watch a TV programme. I got talking to one man who was always cutting himself. He looked like a horror picture with scars everywhere, but underneath the terrible appearance he was actually a nice guy. I really warmed to him, and although I didn't feel the need to cut myself I could understand a bit of why he did it. He didn't do drugs or alcohol, but sometimes his emotional state was so bad that cutting himself was the only way to let the pain out – then, for a while, he didn't feel anything. His appearance was really dreadful: landlords would ask him to leave their pub because the customers were scared of him. Once someone tried to pick a fight with him and he just said, "Come on, then, look at this," and he took a blade and started cutting his arm. The other bloke backed off, afraid, when he saw the blood run down. If someone was prepared to do that to himself, what might he do to you?

That man just didn't care about anything. I could understand that: when no one cares about you, you don't care about yourself. There had been times in my life when I didn't much care if I lived or died. I thought I'd escaped from that sort of despair once, but yet again here I was at the bottom of the pile. What hope was there now that anyone would ever take an interest in me?

# Chapter 5

# GOD'S CHILD

ONE DAY I WAS WALKING into town as usual, to see if I could get a job. On the way I passed a church with a strange sign outside. It said "Jesus is here, come and meet him this Sunday!" I thought this was a really weird thing to say. "Guest appearance of Jesus this Sunday," I thought. "I've heard about God, but appearing in person? That's ridiculous! Anyway, I'm definitely not going to church." Just then a big skinhead character came up to me and said, "OK John? How's things with you?" My first thought was "He's a Londoner – they call everyone John." But then he said, "You know, John, Jesus loves you."

That stopped me in my tracks. Someone had said those very words to me once before, when I was in the hospital. That was really weird – as if God was trying to speak to me. I dismissed the thought as unlikely. Maybe this big guy really did know me. He was a huge bloke as well as being a skinhead, so I wasn't going to get into any arguments with him. If he'd said two and two makes nine I would have said, "Yeah, mate, whatever you say." I have to admit that although he was big he didn't look aggressive, and I could see in his eyes that he was completely sincere. Then I noticed a group of young people standing on the pavement behind him. One of them started playing a keyboard, and they all started singing. I didn't know the song, but the music brought a lump into my throat. They all looked so happy, a group of friends doing something together – though quite what they thought they were doing, singing in the street, I didn't know. They didn't seem to be busking. The big guy gave me a leaflet, and I stuffed it into my pocket and walked away.

When you've lived on the streets as long as I have, you get to know people by how they look at you. You soon learn who the pickpockets are, the drug addicts, the prostitutes, and so on. This lot certainly didn't look dangerous, just young and fresh and sincere. I could tell – living on the streets gives you a Master's degree in life. You know what goes on better than anyone else – you have to, if you're going to survive. I knew that when you're living on the streets you can end up one of two ways: dead, and a statistic, or a fighter. You fight to carry on living, and boy, what fights I'd had!

My body was bruised, battered and scarred from fighting – sometimes literally fighting for my life – but I was even more damaged by psychological battles. All those years as a loner had left me with no sense of worth and no identity of my own. I was always running over things in my mind, reliving the latest bit of pain. At one stage I thought I'd won the fight to go straight: I'd had a job, a home and a wife, and I'd achieved all this by my own strength of character, but then I'd lost that fight and with it everything I valued. I still couldn't see where I'd gone

John as a child:
"Sometimes I wondered why I didn't have a Mum and Dad."

Tadcaster Grammar School. "A stable environment and I really enjoyed it there."

Tadcaster Breweries: "We got over a fence at the back and found loads of reject beer cans."

The viaduct that John dived from when he was a Barnardo's boy.

John visits his mother's grave: "I wish I could have told her how much I needed her, to cry with, to hug, to love."

John and Gillian with their two daughters, Leah and Natalie.

The Eden bus: "the bus was magnificent."

John and his colleague Wayne.

Brenda Sloggett on the bus.

Youngsters on the bus: "the Eden buses are like mobile youth centres ... a good resource for all the young people in these deprived areas of Manchester, not just those who may get into trouble – they're a good place if you just want to chill out with your mates."

Volunteer helpers on the bus.

Members of the Eden bus team with Iain Duncan Smith, Conservative leader, centre; John, third from left; and Andy Hawthorne, director of The Message, second from right.

wrong. All I'd ever wanted was someone to love me and make me feel I was a real person, and now the skinhead's words woke up this terrible longing. "John, Jesus loves you. John, Jesus loves you." It kept echoing in my mind. I needed love, but how could I get it from Jesus? And I needed other things, as well: a home, a job, some friends and a reason for living. Jesus couldn't provide all that. I'd read in my Gideon Bible that he was poor and had no home and no money – if he couldn't do it for himself, how could he fix it for me? "There isn't any truth in all this stuff," I thought, "it's just another big con." No one had ever loved me for myself, and no one ever would.

That night I sat on my bed at the hostel and looked at the sad, hopeless people all around me. Most of them also had awful stories: families who'd rejected them, relationships that had broken down, friends that had betrayed them. No wonder most of them lived in a haze of alcohol or drugs. There wasn't anything else that helped. I settled down for another weary night, with no hope of anything better in the morning. Yet the next day I found myself back in the street where I'd met the big guy, hanging around outside the church and hoping he'd be there again. He was, and he came over to me.

"Do you want to come to this meeting?" he asked. "Clive Calver's going to be speaking."

I had no idea who Clive Calver was, and I certainly didn't fancy going into a church. Where I came from, churchgoers didn't go up to people in the street to get them to come to meetings. Maybe they belonged to some weird cult! The guy told me his name was Tony, and said the meeting wasn't in the church – it was in the Town Hall. That sounded a bit better. I still hesitated, but there was something convincing about him. I didn't say anything as I walked away, but I thought I might go. If I went in late, after the meeting had started, I could sit at the back and not be noticed.

That night I slipped into the back of the Town Hall, very conscious of my shabby clothes, my shaved head and battered shoes, but no one noticed me – they were all looking at the platform at the front of the hall. I found a seat and tried to see what was going on. I was quite pleased to see a table up there, with a loaf of bread and some wine on it. "This can't be bad," I thought. "Perhaps they serve soup as well." There was a lot of singing and some girls were dancing, and everyone seemed happy. I was surprised at that – I'd always thought anything to do with church must be serious and solemn. I thought, "All these people laughing and singing must be completely off the wall. Better be careful – they're nutters in here!" All the same, I wouldn't have minded being as happy as they looked. I had a reputation for being cheerful and cracking jokes, but underneath I was miserable.

Clive Calver stood up and began to speak. I didn't understand some of the words he used, but all at once he started pointing at me and said loudly, "Take off your dirty clothes and give them to God." I was really angry and embarrassed: I was going to get up and shout, "He's having a go at me, what's he need to do that for? My clothes aren't that dirty!" Then I realised he wasn't pointing at me. All in a flash I understood:

he meant all the dirty clothes of misery I wore all the time, the pain, rejection, anger, the sense of betrayal and the terrible loneliness. If I gave them all to God he could heal me. He was offering me everything I wanted: a chance to put things right, a chance to be happy, a chance to let God love me. I stood there at the back of the meeting and thought, "God, I want to be a Christian. I want to get to know you, though I don't know how. But if all this isn't true, I can't handle it. If you're not really there, I'm going to go outside and walk under a bus. After everything I've been through, this has got to be true or I can't go on."

I closed my eyes and prayed. "If you're there, Jesus, I want you to come into my life. I'm sorry for all the wrong things I've done." As I prayed, I felt as if a heavy rucksack had fallen off my shoulders. For the first time it felt as if some of the pain and hurt was being healed. I felt warm all over, and tears started streaming down my face. I still had my eyes closed, but I felt as if I could see a bright light, and I knew that I was forgiven, for everything. I stood there in that hall, rough and grubby in my old clothes, and I felt as if God was saying, "John, you're special to me."

It was a fantastic feeling. I thought, "I've been stabbed and beaten and hurt in the past, and people have robbed stuff off me, but no one can take this away." I knew that I could be killed tomorrow, but still nothing could change what had happened that day. I didn't have to feel worthless and useless any more. Jesus died for me and I was special to him. I can't remember much else that Clive Calver said, because I was busy with my own thoughts. The people all round me noticed that I was standing there with tears running down my face, and some girls came over and gave me a hug. That was fine, but when some of the blokes started hugging me too, I wasn't so keen. They just laughed. I sat there for the rest of the meeting in a warm glow. I still didn't understand everything the speaker was talking about, but I knew he was talking to me. God loved me. I belonged to someone at last.

At the end, I walked back to the hostel humming under my breath, with a big silly grin on my face. I couldn't help it, I just felt happy, as if a pain I'd had for a long time had suddenly gone. When I went into the reception area the staff on duty saw me grinning at everyone and said, "Been drinking, John?"

"No, no," I replied, "I've been to a church meeting." They didn't look as if they believed me. Next morning I was still cheerful, and started singing, "Shine, Jesus, shine" in the dormitory. The hostel staff couldn't cope with it! They said "You're not on drugs, you haven't been drinking, you seem pretty happy. You can look for somewhere else to live." At first I said I needed to stay because I had nowhere else to go, but I left soon afterwards. I put my few possessions in my rucksack, went out and started walking into town again.

"Well," I thought as I walked, "you've got some sense of humour, God. I've just become a Christian and because of that I'm homeless again." Then a car pulled up alongside me, and I saw Tony in the driving seat. He wound down the window and said, "Do you need a place to stay? You can come and live with us, if you like." I was gobsmacked. Why would anyone make me an offer like that? He didn't even know me – and if he had known where I'd been and some of the things I'd done, he certainly wouldn't have asked me! I was a bit wary at first. I thought, "There has to be a catch. Maybe they'll kidnap me, or else I'll be doing the washing up for two years here." Still, what did I have to lose? In the end I gave in and said, "OK, I'll give it a go."

Tony and his wife Sylvia lived in an ordinary house, but it looked wonderful to me: clean and homely after the squalid surroundings of the hostel. I had a room of my own with a quilt on the bed and a fresh-smelling pillow – the clean bedding looked lovely after the stained, grubby, smelly bed I was used to. I put my rucksack down on the bedroom floor and looked around, but I didn't dare to touch anything. Then I went downstairs and stood in the hall. I could hear voices in the living room, but I didn't know if I could go in – I felt like a nervous puppy, waiting all the time for someone to tell me I'd done something wrong. The fact was that I'd been living on the fringes of ordinary life for so long, I didn't know how to behave any more. Then the living-room door opened and Tony came out and saw me. "Come on in, John, and sit down," he said. "Cup of tea?" I could hardly believe what was happening.

Overnight I'd gone from scavenging in bins to having someone give me regular meals; from sleeping in a dirty, noisy dormitory to sleeping in my own room; from wandering around on my own to having a family to live with and talk to. It was fantastic. I loved sitting round the dinner table, having a talk over a meal. It felt friendly and homely, and I loved the great debates we had on every subject under the sun. Tony and Sylvia's son was in the army, and they welcomed me into their home as if I was another son. They were like the loving foster parents I'd never had, but I'd always been looking for.

They knew what they were taking on, though, and they knew it wouldn't be easy for any of us. They said, "You'll have to learn how to live with us as we go along. If you nick the car or get into trouble we'll have to sort it out together – but we won't throw you out." Nobody in my life had ever said, "If you get it wrong we'll still love you." I thought love was something you grabbed when it was around because it didn't last long. I did try them out a bit, because I needed to see if they really could love me. I went out one night and got really drunk, came in late and was sick on the floor. All they said was, "We still love you, John, but you've got to clear up the mess yourself." They were amazing. They really lived out the gospel of love, and they showed me how to understand God's unconditional love for us. It was almost too big an idea for me to take in.

I stayed with Tony and Sylvia for about a year. Living in their home taught me how to live with other people as a family, and going to church with them taught me more about my faith. I'll never forget them because their love and care helped to transform my life. Gradually my rough edges were being chipped away. It couldn't have been easy for them, because when they took me in I was in a terrible state. I was covered in tattoos and scars, my clothes were dirty and my jeans were torn. I knew the meaning of holiness, but only because I had holes in my jacket and trainers! I must have looked like a stray dog that needed a good home. My emotional state wasn't much better, and it took a while before I started to learn that I could trust them.

Tony was the pastor of a house church that been set up by the Ichthus Christian Fellowship, a Christian group based in London. My first experiences of worship were with that little group of Christians, but the church had links with South Street Baptist Church in Deptford, and after a while Tony and Sylvia started taking me up to attend big meetings there. I'd never seen anything like it: huge balconies filled with hundreds of Christians. The atmosphere was amazing – great music, beautiful singing, and the preaching was so down-to-earth that even I, with my basic understanding of the Bible, could understand it all right. There were all kinds of people there, reflecting the mixed community in the area – black, white, Asian, oriental; people with disabilities and from all walks of life. There was a real feeling of acceptance and love, and a sense of the presence of God. I started going to their meetings regularly as well as to the local church.

All the time my life and my attitudes were changing. It wasn't easy, and I struggled with myself a lot of the time. I knew I was right at the start of a new way of life, and I had a lot to learn. But in return, being a Christian was giving me so much. I'd started to feel a new sense of peace, and I knew that nothing could ever take it away from me. I knew life wasn't going to be all sunshine from now on: there would still be troubles and disappointments and difficulties, but I knew that at least God was with me through it all. When I said to God, "I want to be a Christian" I didn't know anything about Christian teaching. I didn't know any of the Christian in-words – I thought that "ecumenical" sounded like a brand of washing machine! When people asked me "What denomination are you?" I'd say, "I'm a Christian."

I started to get involved with what Tony and Sylvia were doing – going out onto the streets and helping other people who'd hit rock bottom like me. Along with the Ichthus Christian Fellowship I got involved with presenting the love of God in drama and music, creating openings to start conversations with people who didn't know anything about the gospel. I also started studying – the first reading and discussion that I'd done since I left school ten years before. The leaders of the Network team in Deptford were people like Roger Forster and Roger Mitchell, who were really good teachers. Alongside our practical experience of work on the streets, they provided teaching on discipleship to back it up. Sometimes we talked about drugs, alcohol, divorce, and all the other things that damage people's lives, and that was difficult for me, because I was still sensitive about lots of things. Sometimes my tears were very near the surface as I talked about what effect those things had had on my own life, but I felt safe and protected with my new friends around me and praying with me. I had a lot of help: I made some great friendships within the Fellowship, and they became the brothers and sisters I'd always wanted. The change in me gave me a burning passion to share the love of Jesus with other people. I knew it could transform lives.

I got involved in soup runs, helping the homeless in the East End's "cardboard city". One day I met a girl who was on hundreds of pounds' worth of heroin and temazepam daily; she had a pimp as a boyfriend, and was terminally ill with HIV. I was shocked when I realised how easily I could have gone down a similar route. I knew the first stages of that road, and I wanted to protect her and other young people from the despair that could make them seek escape through drugs.

Another day I found myself sitting on a train with a man who was grubby and smelt of drink. I felt as if God was saying to me, "Tell him how special he is." I could see he was very drunk, but I went ahead and started telling him that God loved him. In my bag I had a little teddy bear with a cross attached to it. I wasn't going to show him the teddy (I had my street cred to think of!) but I put my hand in my bag and took the cross off and gave it to him. He looked at me in confusion and then down at the cross in his hand; then he closed his fingers over it and put it in his pocket. His eyes filled with tears and I could see he was touched by being given something by a stranger. I knew that he probably wouldn't remember much about what I'd said. But the next day, when he put his hand in his pocket, he'd find that cross.

At the end of the course the leaders of the Ichthus Fellowship asked me if I wanted to be baptised. I was really keen – I wanted to show the world that I was accepted by Jesus and I wanted to follow him all my life. Being baptised was an emotional experience for me, the chance to do something to show how serious I was about being a Christian. It was great to have all my friends waiting to welcome me as I came up out of the water.

The one thing I was sure of was that I wanted to serve God as best I could. Over the fence at the back of Tony and Sylvia's house there was a gypsy camp which I could see from my bedroom window. I felt close to the gypsy families because I could identify with them: they lived on the fringes of society rather like I used to, and they often found it hard to be accepted or to find anyone willing to help them. I used to go and visit them, making friends and telling them about Jesus and what he'd done for me. I specially liked talking to the children – I loved sharing my new-found faith with the kids.

Once when I was chatting with a gypsy family the Mum told me about something that had happened to them. Their little boy came home from school with a picture of Jesus and two angels, and said, "Look at this picture, Mum: that angel on the left is me." She said, "Don't be silly, that isn't you." Later that day he crossed the road and was killed by a passing car. It was just as if he was telling his Mum, "I'm going to be with Jesus." That picture was a great comfort to her as she came to terms with her terrible loss. There were a lot of Christian gypsies on the site who really loved God, and although they still had their financial difficulties and various hassles, their strong faith helped them. Two particular friends of mine were Joey and Bridie, and they helped me understand more about gypsy life. We used to sit round their campfire talking, praying together and sharing meals, and they treated me like one of their own.

Tony had his own business as a contract gardener, and he used to take me out with him so I could earn a bit of pocket money cutting grass. It felt really good to be able to earn some money honestly, by working hard. I took a pride in doing a good job, and I liked having money of my own again. I still had to learn, however, about giving money for God's work. One day I was sitting in a church when I felt God saying, "Share your money with me, John." I only had a £10 note, and I really had to struggle to make myself give it away. I stuffed it in a collection box in the church. Two days later I got a letter from the Inland Revenue, who'd finally caught up with me, enclosing a tax rebate of £300. That was when I realised that God has a sense of humour!

Part of my work with the Ichthus Christian Fellowship involved a mission to France. It was a real adventure with a group of good friends – very different from my sad and lonely trip across the Channel a couple of years before. We travelled in an old minibus, taking the ferry to Calais and driving on to Lille; the weather was warm, and on the way we slept out on benches in our sleeping bags. We were helping a church in a little village, and we stayed in a large house nearby, meeting local Christians and sharing in their worship. I still remember the warmth of the people and the feeling of fellowship as we sang and

prayed together each day. Each team had an inter-
preter. We visited blocks of flats and knocked on
doors, telling people who we were and why we'd
come, and inviting them to our meetings, where we
prayed and offered drama presentations. I was
thrilled to see people coming to know Jesus through
the mission, and I was filled with admiration for the
more experienced Christians in our group. I wanted
so much to be like them. I'd been reading all the
Nicky Cruz books and I wanted to copy him, but I
knew that wasn't right. I could feel God saying to me,
"John, I don't want you to be a Nicky Cruz or anybody
else. I'll use you just as you are; I want John Robinson
to work for me."

We had a lot of fun in France. I loved the countryside, the weather, the scent of the wild flowers,
and especially the food – cheeses and crisp French
bread and wine at meals. The rest of the team teased
me about my broad Yorkshire accent, so I told them I
had a job understanding them, too. I learned a lot
from the various speakers at our meetings, and I
knew I was growing through the good Bible teaching
and the experience of mission. When it was time for
us to go home, I begged to be allowed to stay a little
longer: I didn't want the adventure to end. I stayed on
and paid my way by doing some painting in the village, and treating the wooden outhouses. I even managed to share my testimony with the students at a
local college, with someone to translate for me as my
French still wasn't very good.

There was one lovely Christian girl who was part
of the mission team, and I fell madly in love with her.

For a while I had great hopes of this relationship, but after a while I realised that it wasn't to be: I was attracted to her for all the wrong reasons. I was still only a young Christian, and I had lots of lessons to learn, especially about what real love involves. God was able to teach me a lot through this rather precipitous friendship; in particular, I had to learn how to be unselfish and how to avoid hurting other people. It was perhaps the first failure of a relationship that I had ever been able to accept without bitterness or resentment. My time in France wasn't wasted. I came home a better person.

# Chapter 6

# A NEW LIFE

BACK IN ENGLAND I REALISED that although life was much better for me now, I still had lots of problems and some deep emotional scars. I'd had a lifetime of rejection, and the pressure inside me from that was huge. It was like a bottle of lemonade which has been shaken up: if the cap had come off straight away, the pressure would have been too much to bear. God knew what he was doing, and instead was easing the lid off a bit at a time, so the pressure was released in manageable bits, and everything didn't come fizzing over at once. I had a history of pain which needed to come to the surface before my healing could begin. Joey and Bridie had some friends on the Isle of Wight who were good at ministering to people with emotional needs, and they suggested that I should spend some time there. They made the arrangements and took me to the ferry at Portsmouth, prayed with me and waved me off. I was touched that they cared so much about me.

When I arrived in the Isle of Wight I was met by Julie and Ian, who took me into their home. They had two children, Lucy and Chris, and three cats, who went by the names of Peace, Glory and Hallelujah. (When I was asked to call the cats in at night I refused

– can you imagine what the neighbours would say if you stood in the garden shouting "Peace! Glory! Hallelujah!"?) I had a room of my own, but I spent a lot of time with Chris, who was a computer whizz, and had a TV in his room permanently plugged into a computer game called "Bubble Bubble". I used to go off cycling with Lucy, too, though she was always shouting at me to slow down, because I went too fast for her nine-year-old legs to keep up. I was so touched that Julie and Ian trusted me with their daughter. It made me feel like an older brother.

Julie usually did the cooking and made sure we all ate together at meal times – when she called us, we all raced downstairs – but the meals were an eye-opener for me. They were really family times, and anything and everything would be discussed over the dining table. It was lovely to be a part of it.

Settling in and getting to know them was great, but then came the crunch time: they wanted to discuss my problems and see what needed to be addressed – I was going to have to face up to my experiences of rejection and pain. They already had an inkling of my troubles. If I did things wrong, they used to tell me off as freely (and as lovingly) as they did their own children, and they'd seen how fragile I was. Any criticism felt like a total rejection to me. We needed to talk about all this, take it to God, and pray for healing. I lost count of the amount of time I spent in tears in their living room, with Julie and Ian praying with me. I dredged up a lot of past experiences and came to terms with them. It was a safe place to cry out to God, with the support and love of my friends around me.

One day Ian suggested that I should write down the names of all the people who had ever hurt me. It took a long time, as I went over painful events in my past life, and sometimes wrote a little note when I hadn't even known the person's name. Then he asked me to say, "Jim, in Jesus' name I forgive you."

I couldn't do it. I found the names stuck in my throat, so deep was the resentment I felt against some of the people in my life. It took weeks before I could do it, and honestly say that I had forgiven all those people. When I finally got to the end of the list, it was a time of real healing for me.

I was accepted into the local fellowship where Ian was a pastor, and I paid my way by doing some painting and decorating jobs. I was also allowed a taste of leadership, by joining in on the beach missions they held for holidaymakers. I really enjoyed talking to the young people, and I found it easy to get on with them and talk about my faith.

After a while I knew I was ready to move on; dearly though I loved Julie and Ian and their family, I had to become a bit more independent. They agreed, but knew that I still needed quite a lot of support. I wasn't quite ready to strike out alone. Then someone suggested that I might like to work at Lee Abbey, the Christian family and conference centre in north Devon – they were looking for someone to join their community and also to get involved in the work with children and young people. I didn't think they would even consider me for the job, because I didn't exactly look the part. Still, I went for an interview and I was over the moon when they told me they wanted me. I knew that there God would be able to continue the amazing healing work he was doing in me.

By this stage in my Christian life, I had made a lot of friends, but Julie and Ian were something more. They were much more like a family – and not just because Julie took seriously my need for structure in my life, and would tell me off and provide discipline as well as love. Unlike other friends who drifted in and out of my life, Julie and Ian never let me go. Even after I'd moved away they went on caring for me, sending me birthday and Christmas cards and little parcels of treats. Before I left them they took me to Portsmouth to visit the second-hand shops, and bought me a whole new wardrobe of clothes. They didn't have much money, but they shared what they had willingly, and that gesture meant a lot to me. It was hard for me to leave them, and I will always remember what they did for me with gratitude and fondness. They helped me to receive God's healing, and they accepted me into their lives and gave me a taste of honest, real family life.

Lee Abbey is an impressive cream stone building set in beautiful scenery. The fields run down to the sea and on a clear day you can see the Welsh coast. A man called Trevor was appointed to be my mentor, and he showed me round, prayed with me and looked after me generally. At first I felt nervous and uncomfortable – the rest of the community came from a wide variety of backgrounds, and I wasn't sure how I was going to get on with all these different people.

The system at Lee Abbey is an interesting one:

you go there for six weeks initially, and then decide if you want to stay. If you do, you have to make some promises, such as putting other community members before yourself, nurturing your spiritual life and honouring one another. After the six weeks I did feel that it was the right place for me. There were odd times when some of the visiting guests made personal remarks, like "Are you on day release from prison?" I got a bit upset sometimes, but Trevor said, "That's not your problem, it's theirs," and in the end I decided I had to be myself. I have to admit, though, that even I had a mega problem with my tattoos – I thought people were staring at me all the time. It was hard work, too, living and building relationships with about 70 other workers in the community. If the people on the Big Brother programme on telly think they've got it hard, then they should try living at Lee Abbey! Living alongside so many other people made it quite wacky at times, but I was very happy there.

I took my place working in the teams – sometimes in the house, sometimes in the grounds, and sometimes with the guests. I specially loved working outside in the estate grounds: the views were beautiful. I enjoyed the life there, but I had painful times at birthdays and Christmas. All my life I'd watched other people getting cards and presents and visits from family and friends, and I'd grown to hate those special days, because I just couldn't stop myself from feeling lonely and miserable. Nowadays I had Julie and Ian who always sent me a card or phoned me, but I still felt a twinge of sadness that I didn't have a family of my own. Without those two, I wouldn't have had anyone.

Sometimes when it was quiet, or at a weekend when it was changeover from one week's guests to the next, some of us would go down to the pub. I was amused by how different it was from the old days: now it was just a few friends having a quiet drink. However, we didn't get a lot of free time, and mostly we were very busy, because thousands of people came to stay at Lee Abbey each year.

One of my main jobs was working with the young people. I used to show them the film *The Cross and the Switchblade* and share the story of my experiences with them afterwards. Lots of these kids came from quite different backgrounds from mine, but they seemed to relate to me easily, and I loved working with them. Other bits of my job I found harder – my paperwork was always a bit out of control – but the activities with the young people, the Bible readings and times of prayer were something special. Sometimes we used to go up to the tower on the hill to look at the view, then walk down to the beach and play games, light a bonfire and sing. I used to get letters from these kids saying how much they enjoyed their stay. I realised that I had a gift for this, and the Warden seemed to think so too – he always arranged for me to work with that age group.

Other parts of my life were going more smoothly, too, and I knew God was continuing to heal me. I learned patience and understanding and how to listen to people. I learned how to look for God's will and to put it before what I wanted to do. It took time for me to learn how to handle relationships with some of the other community workers, but it was a valuable time of development in every area of my life. Sometimes there were disagreements and I fell out with people, but I was learning how to control my irritation, and how to make up after an argument. It was all part of the growing process.

One of the best things for me was that I never felt lonely now. At Lee Abbey I was surrounded by friends. There was a special couple called Rodney and Margo, who were like an uncle and aunt to me. They had a toothless black and white cat called Bruce, who used to follow me when I went for a walk. I'd be sitting on a rock in the valley, admiring the view across the sea, and then I'd feel a wet nudge on my hand and there was Bruce, a mile away from home, keeping me company with a lick. If I shooed him away he came back and tried to bite me – those toothless bites used to make me laugh, even when I was talking to God. Margo and Rodney had a great sense of humour coupled with an amazing sensitivity. They could tell when I felt depressed or upset, and they knew how to get alongside me, sometimes to correct and teach me, or else to encourage me when the going was tough.

Another one of the community, Paul Webster, became one of my best friends, and has remained one ever since. Paul worked on the estate full-time with his friends, Hilton and Rob, and I joined them once a week on the log run. Paul was the first friend I'd had who was prepared to share his life's experiences with me, and we prayed and shed a few tears together. Later on he was Best Man at my wedding, and I was

Best Man for both him and Rob. Hilton and Rob were good at keeping my feet on the ground and they became wonderful Christian brothers to me.

One evening when I was serving the guests at the dining table there was a prison chaplain talking about crime and prisons. She talked at some length, saying that in her view, everyone who was in prison deserved to be there. She really seemed to have no time for anyone who'd been in prison. I rolled up my sleeves so she could see my tattoos as I came over to clear the dishes, and she said, "They're interesting." Once we'd got into conversation I said, "I was one of those prisoners you were talking about, but I didn't know any better. I don't believe God thinks prisoners deserve what they get. He loves them and knows they've got it wrong, but he forgives them and tries to help them see their way. Some people end up in prison just because they never had a good stable home life where they could be taught right and wrong." I really hoped I wasn't offending her, but I felt very strongly about it. Comments like hers can set someone back years when they're trying to straighten out their life again. I felt a bit bruised by her attitude, but in my quiet times of Bible reading and prayer I used to take all these things to God.

Lee Abbey gave me a loan so I could buy a bike, and that gave me the freedom to explore much further afield, so I could go right out into the hills and be on my own. I remember one night there was a full moon, and I was sitting on the cliff looking out over the sea. The water was sparkling in the moonlight and I gazed at the beauty of God's creation. I felt that

God was saying to me, "This is a beautiful world. This is how I created it. Don't worry about anything. Trust me completely and I'll teach you more and more about me." I went away with peace in my heart.

I was always sharing my testimony. I was so excited by my new-found faith that I couldn't keep quiet about it, but being so open about myself meant that I could also be hurt. I knew I had to be careful how I behaved, and Mike Edson, the Warden of Lee Abbey, kept an eye on me. He encouraged me to take responsibility and lovingly corrected me, and his fatherly influence helped to knock off a few more of my rough edges. I still went too far sometimes. During one prayer meeting I hid a wind machine under someone's chair and as they began to pray I pressed the button on the remote control and a very strange noise erupted! I was in hysterics, but the person involved went bright red and all the others tried hard to keep straight faces. They told me gently that this wasn't appropriate for a prayer meeting, and suggested that I tamed my sense of humour. That sort of thing happened a lot in the early days. Once I played some practical jokes and I was called to the office and asked to pay for some of the stuff I'd broken. At first I used to try and make excuses, but Mike would say, "No, don't make excuses, just pay for what you've done. You know we care about you, and we're guiding you the right way." Afterwards I was pleased, because what he said wasn't a rejection, just the correction I needed. It was just like a father training his child.

I didn't get paid a lot – just pocket-money,

because food and lodging was provided and I only had toiletries and cigarettes to buy. I was a bit embarrassed about the cigarettes, but smoking was my one vice. Still, I knew God was dealing with it, so I relaxed about it. I felt a wonderful sense of peace with God, even about the things I knew still needed sorting out in my life. I used to be so happy, whistling as I worked on the estate, filling my little dumper truck with logs and delivering them to the houses. I thought, "This is the right relationship to have with God. You're protected, you're learning his lessons, and you're loved and cared for as his son."

Lee Abbey is a wonderful place and in a sense it was like God's hospital for me. I felt him healing me in so many areas. At Lee Abbey, you couldn't say, "I'm fine" if you weren't. Someone would soon notice. It was such a tightly-knit, loving community. All the good in me, and the bad and the ugly had to come to the surface and be sorted out. It was really hard for me to think about my past – I'd hated the old John – but I was learning that I had a good side, too, that was caring and loving. God put these good things into my heart. Lots of visitors to the Abbey had awful problems; it was a privilege to be a listener for them, and show them the love of Christ that I'd found.

I spent nearly two years at Lee Abbey, and during that time I made lots of real and lasting friends, but I always hated it when people moved on. I'd had enough of losing people in my life, and I always cried when good friends left. One member of staff was a nun called Sister Carol. I used to tease her and say, "Well, you're a nun, so there's nun of this and nun of that and certainly nun of the other!" She wasn't offended, and just laughed – she knew I was just being me. Sister Carol was wonderful when I was upset: a good listener who seemed to understand my feelings. Her faith was so strong and real, it helped to build me up.

It was a great place to grow as a Christian: I didn't just learn from the speakers and teachers, but from living in fellowship with other Christians. I wasn't a very good timekeeper, and one day I was asked to take the lead at prayer time, but I wasn't prepared. Mike Edson took me aside and pointed out that Jesus had died on the cross for me – the least I could do in return was to get up for prayer time. It was invaluable to be reminded of the value of prayer in the Christian life.

For a while it had been good for me just to have friendships, but even though I had lovely brothers and sisters now, I still wished I could have someone of my own. When I first met Gillian she was staying at Lee Abbey for a couple of months as a "working guest" – someone who lives and works alongside the community but who isn't a permanent part of it. We used to go for long walks on the hills and on the beach and gradually got to know each other well. I began to realise that this was more than just another friendship – Gillian was special. Something we had in common was a deep sense of vocation and a desire to work for God. Gillian had known from the age of fourteen that God wanted her to be ordained as a minister, though at that time she'd attended a church where they didn't agree with the ordination of women. It had been years before she'd realised that it really was a possibility. Meanwhile she'd gone to university in Edinburgh and taken a degree in Divinity, and went on to serve God as a lay worker, working as a minister in a church.

I wanted to ask her out to dinner, but I didn't have any money, so on our first date we went out for a drive in her car instead. On the way back I told her that I wanted to kiss her, but I wasn't going to unless she said that she was serious about me! I was so worried about being hurt yet again if I let myself love someone, but deep down we both knew that the feelings we had for each other were very special.

Gillian's time at Lee Abbey came to an end and she went back to Southampton. After only six weeks we knew we wanted to get married. We were very happy, but I'm not sure her parents saw it in quite the same light. Gillian says she went home and told her dad that she'd met this really amazing bloke and she was going to marry him, but in her enthusiasm everything tumbled out at once: "He's a Christian and he's covered in tattoos, and he's had a really rotten upbringing and he's been in prison and he's fantastic!" I wondered why he was a bit quiet the first time I met him. Still, once we'd got to know each other we got on really well.

At last I knew it was time to move on again, time to take up my responsibilities in the real world. I'd learned a lot – especially the need to discipline myself – but most of all I knew with absolute certainty that Jesus would walk with me every day and be my constant companion. This gave me the courage to start yet another phase of my life. I said good bye to all my much-loved friends at Lee Abbey and promised to keep in touch with them. I'd done a lot of growing as a Christian there, and God had got rid of a lot more of my rough edges. I left with a fiancée who loved me, and a new purpose. I knew what God wanted me to do: to help other young people who'd fallen on bad times like me. I asked God to lead me and to help me to serve him wholeheartedly.

# Chapter 7

# STREETWISE

WE STARTED MAKING PLANS for our wedding. We were looking forward to inviting all our friends to be with us in church when we made our vows before God, so it was a terrible shock when the vicar of St Andrew's Church (Gillian's boss) told us it wasn't going to happen like that.

"I can't marry you in this church," he said, "because John's been married before. I can give you a blessing in church, though."

I was horrified. I was a Christian, and I knew that God had forgiven my past, yet I still wasn't allowed to get married in church. It felt like another rejection – this time from the church, the Christian people I thought I could trust. I felt guilty, too, that I was robbing Gillian of something she deserved – a full wedding in church in front of God. I felt really angry for a while, but in the end we accepted the facts. We both knew that whether the ceremony took place in a Registry Office or a church, it was what we were saying to each other and to God that really mattered. We knew God was there as we said a prayer in the Registry Office, and we knew that our life ahead was to be a triple relationship, with God at the centre.

We had a wonderful wedding day: about two

hundred people came to share our joy. There were Gillian's friends and family, friends from Lee Abbey, and Simeon and John, two wonderful musicians. They played "Such love" and "With our feet on the rock". After the formalities in the Registry Office we had a blessing in the church. My day was made when I watched Gillian coming up the aisle with her Dad. We held the reception in the New Forest and drove through it in a splendid car, waving at the horses and feeling we were royalty! We were Prince and Princess in God's eyes, and that was all that mattered. Then we set off on our honeymoon (two weeks in Gran Canaria, a generous present from a friend): we were Mr and Mrs Robinson!

When we came back down to earth we discussed our future plans. I'd been asked to conduct a survey about why young people didn't attend church. I also knew without a trace of doubt that I must be involved in outreach in my own locality, getting to know young people who were taking drugs, who were lonely or angry, and getting into trouble with the police. I wanted to contact young people who had no knowledge of God and no connections with the church.

The results of the survey were interesting. Most of the young people I contacted in schools and youth clubs said that church was boring and out of touch. They didn't believe that the church had anything to say that could be relevant to them. I wrote a 50-page report for the New Forest churches, because I knew that lots of them really wanted to know how they could help. I was helping with the youth programme in the same church where Gillian worked as a lay worker, and I told the youngsters about all the wonderful things God had done in my life. Even in the better areas, where there were big houses and tree-lined streets, the same old troubles lurked beneath the surface. I was amazed to find that even there, many of the young people felt rejected. They seemed to have everything, but they were still bored and lonely.

Lots of churches wanted to work with young people, but they didn't have the resources. I had a vision: to take the gospel onto the streets instead of expecting the young people to come into church. To do that I needed a vehicle, but I didn't have any money to buy one. At the time I was earning a living as a care worker in a special school for children with emotional and behavioural difficulties. I was frustrated by the work, because it was a secular organisation, and so I couldn't share the gospel with the kids as I would have liked to do. Still, it paid me a salary – enough to live on, but not enough to buy a van for outreach.

All the same, I started hunting around for a suitable vehicle, and when I found a camper van I was delighted. I looked inside and saw that it had curtains, nice seats, a sink with taps, and a little toilet. If this could be kitted out with a place to sit and talk and somewhere to make hot drinks, it would be perfect. To my delight and surprise, the Bishop of Winchester decided to support the project, and arranged the finances to enable me to buy the van.

I knew I needed a team of people behind me, so I

visited several local churches and told them about my ideas for outreach, and recruited teams of people to help. Then I drove around and assessed the areas I wanted to work in. I started chatting to the kids and building up relationships with them. I also contacted the police and other agencies – youth workers, counsellors, schools and so on – so that they knew what I was doing. I trained the teams of helpers, too, because they needed to know about Child Protection laws, and anger management techniques, and lots of other things to enable them to help the young people.

The van went down well. Young people wanted someone to talk to – and a warm place to sit. There were loads of opportunities to get to know them and find out about the kind of things they were worried about. Some of the local papers did features on the work, writing headlines like, "Ex-con, ex-Barnardo's boy helps his own." I didn't think much of the headlines, but they got people interested in what we were doing, and brought in more support.

Lots of people gave their time to help us, including a woman called Janet Hallpatch, who handled a lot of the paperwork, let us use her house for meetings, and gave us a huge amount of support. As more churches got involved, more money came in (enough to repair the van and pay me a wage) and we even appointed a chairperson and secretary. We called the outreach "Streetwise" and painted the name on the van. Janet and her family treated me like one of their own. They are a fantastic family.

That ancient camper van was held together by chewing gum and a prayer! It always needed repairs because it was in constant use. In the evenings, at weekends and in school holidays we'd be out in all weathers, driving round the back streets of Dibden and Hythe. We'd hear the kids say, "Here comes the God bus!" and they always seemed pleased to see us. Some of the clergy who came out with me were amazed at what God was doing in some of the areas – they were shocked, too, at some of the sights we saw. We'd get talking to the kids and offer them a hot drink and a place to sit in the warm and out of the rain. After a while they'd get to know us and start to confide in us and tell us about themselves. Some of their stories were painful to hear: some of them had been abused, others had alcohol or drug problems, or tried to find affection by sleeping around. Lots of them, though, were just ordinary kids – they didn't have any special problems, but they were bored and didn't have much to do except hang around the streets with their mates. As they came to trust us some of them asked why we put so much effort into helping them. Then we were able to tell them about Jesus, and they listened to what we had to say. Several of them became Christians.

The police came and checked out the project, and thought the work we were doing was good – they often came and worked alongside us, taking their chance to talk to the kids in a relaxed and non-confrontational situation.

All this time I had held onto my childhood dream that one day I'd find my Mum. I used to imagine it in detail: I'd knock on her door and she'd open it with rollers in her hair and a Woodbine in her hand! I always thought of the house as having net curtains and flowers in the widow – a picture of ordinary, pleasant homeliness and security. She'd say, "Hi, John, come in," as if it was an everyday thing. And she'd be pleased to see me.

Now I was married, I felt strong enough to go and look for that dream, because I had Gillian to go with me. I thought that at the same time I could go and visit some of the places where I'd grown up, and show Gillian. I was really excited that I had someone interested enough to come and visit my childhood places with me.

One thing that had always annoyed me was the thought that the local authority must have known about the abuse in those foster homes, but they did nothing about it. No wonder kids in care kicked against the system; they knew there was no one who was prepared to protect them. I'd decided a few years earlier that I wanted to see my Social Services records, and the law now said that these had to be made available to adults. They made fascinating reading. I was pleased in a way, because they clarified things that were only hazy memories, or that I hadn't understood before. I found that my brother Kenneth was a year older than me and we'd been placed together in the foster home where he died. There had always seemed to be a lot of children there: now I saw that five of us were fostered and two had been adopted. How much the social workers really knew about the situation remains unclear. My notes say that when I was nine I wouldn't go to school "because he doesn't like it". Only I and the foster parents knew that I sometimes didn't go to school because I'd been locked in the cellar – not something that was likely to appear in case notes without urgent action resulting.

Seeing the bald facts of my childhood recorded, and reading the comments in various social workers' reports on me, reduced Gillian to tears. She was angry that such superficial knowledge of a child could be set down as facts in documents that followed me from home to home throughout my young life. Many of the comments were contradictory: "He never shows any feeling for anyone"; "a willing helper who will readily help anyone in need". Other comments refer to behaviour that nowadays would (one hopes) set alarm bells ringing: apparently I used to take food and hide it (common among children who are never sure if food will be withheld), and "collected things like a magpie". At one stage I'd had an eye test but was found not to need glasses: "the doctor said this could be an emotional rather than a physical problem." Even the bedwetting was ignored, although I would think that bedwetting at the age of nine was unusual enough to suggest emotional problems.

In fact it was only when I was assessed at the Kanner Unit that anyone seems to have attempted to understand what was going on: "We feel that he is extremely insecure in his relationships and this is why he is so sensitive to reprimand... It is not surprising that a boy such as John who has had a long and unsatisfactory fostering experience is unable to accept that he isn't missing out." Had someone finally seen that something was badly wrong, not just with me, but with the situation they'd placed me in? Was it the case that overworked social workers were unable to take the time to look at the problems, and had complete faith in the version of events given them by the adults? Or did someone have suspicions at last? I'll never know, but it's hardly surprising that as I grew up I sometimes felt as if everyone was against me. It must have felt as if all the adults were in league together.

The Barnardo's reports are generally more sympathetic; at least they saw me all the time, not for brief visits. They noted things like "John is still trying to find an identity... needs a great deal of affection and understanding." There are little verbal snapshots: "a likeable boy", "enjoys swimming", "holds his food in two hands like a squirrel", "a boy you could rely on in an emergency", "John likes school and does his homework quite happily". It looks as though the security of the Barnardo's home was slowly undoing the damage of the early years.

There are references throughout the notes to the lack of contact with my family. The meeting with my older brother was recorded – he was mentioned later as being in Borstal. I wrote letters to my older sister, and was upset when I didn't get a reply. A note about my mother says that she was willing to see one of my older brothers, "but she never mentions John". When I was fifteen a social worker wrote: "I expected John to bring up the subject of his family and thought he might revert to the idea of seeing his brothers. This time, however, he talked about his mother and talked wistfully of wanting a photograph of her." No such thing was forthcoming, and the social workers persuaded me not to try to trace her until I was 18, when they thought I might be better able to "cope with the experience of meeting her". They were probably trying to protect me from yet more rejection; anyway, it never happened. I spent my eighteenth birthday in Borstal.

Now I felt it was time to go back, and we set off to visit Barnardo's at Tadcaster. I was over the moon when one of the staff remembered me. "You've grown up, John," she said, "but I never forgot your smiling face!" I had tears in my eyes as I walked round my old home. The woods and meadows sloping to the River Wharfe were still the same, the viaduct was still there, and I looked down into the water where we used to dive. My years at Barnardo's had given me happy memories and some security in an otherwise bleak existence.

Gillian was pleased when I said I was going to try to trace my mother, but she thought we were going on some sort of detective trail, trying to look at records and track her down. It was only once we were in Yorkshire that I let on that I knew her name and address, which I'd memorised from writing to her years before. We found the road – a typical Yorkshire street of back-to-back houses – and the right house. As we walked up the path I said to Gillian, "You say something when she opens the door," and she said, "No, *you* say something." I knocked on the door and a young girl opened it.

I asked nervously whether my mother was in.

"No, sorry," the young girl replied. "There was a

woman by that name here, but she died three months ago."

I was stunned. I stood rooted to the spot for a moment, then I just said, "Thanks for your time," and walked away.

We got in the car and Gillian burst into tears. She couldn't bear to see the stunned, defeated look on my face. It was the death of my dream. One day, I'd thought, I would sit and have a cup of tea with my Mum and it would be an ordinary thing, and everything would be all right. That dream had kept me going through all the toughest times of my life, but it was too late now. My Mum was never going to want me. Gillian cried for me, because I couldn't cry. I didn't know what was going on in my mind. I felt as if a piece of me had been cut away. I'd had a mother whom I hadn't known and now she was dead. No one had even notified me of her death. We drove off in silence; I was lost for words.

We went to look for Mum's grave, and found the location from the local undertaker. It was an unmarked plot in a local cemetery. That really upset me – how could someone's life end up as just a numbered plot in the ground? We put a bunch of flowers on it, and when we got home Gillian's Dad helped me to make a simple wooden cross. I carved some words on it: "Mum – I love you – John", and we went back to put it on the grave. In fact, later on we found that a proper headstone had been erected, probably by some of her other children. I had been the last of her eight children by her first husband, and I seem to have been the only one she completely disowned, though several of the others spent time in care, including my brother Kenneth who died there. Later she went on to have four other children by her second husband, and all of those were brought up at home.

Eventually I managed to make some enquiries about Mum's last days, and found that she'd spent them in a hospital in Huddersfield. We managed to trace the Roman Catholic priest who had taken her funeral. He told us that she had spent some time with a nun shortly before her death. I talked to the nun, who was really kind, and she told me that she prayed with my Mum for her sins to be forgiven and that she would know Jesus. I was very comforted by this: the fact that I knew Jesus, and my mother had come to know him too before she died. It took away a burden of worry that had troubled me for many years, and I felt at peace. There didn't seem to be anything I could do now – I'd missed seeing her by only three months.

I returned to the grave several times and left little notes there. It wasn't that I thought my Mum was there, but it was just something I had to do. There were things I'd never got the chance to say to her in life, and I felt the need to be able say them, somehow, now. After that I felt better: as if the room in my heart that I'd kept for her had been cleaned by God and sealed. I did investigate the whereabouts of my Dad, but I drew a blank. If he's alive I wish him well, but I don't feel that I have to try to find him. With my Mum it was different. I like to think she was a courageous woman who must have faced hardships and difficult decisions in her life. The work I do now shows me something of what her life must have been like, having twelve children in difficult circumstances. I believe she didn't contact me because she felt it was better for me to be in care, and I don't feel bitter about it. Yet I wish she had wanted to see me, even just one time, because that rejection is one which runs incredibly deep.

God's love has taught me a lot, and at the end I had nothing but love in my heart for the Mum I never knew. I have enough love now: I know that in God's eyes I'm his special child.

Chapter **8**                    # KEEPING IT
                                 # REAL

MEANWHILE, GILLIAN STILL FELT a strong calling to be ordained. We spent a lot of time praying about our future together, and we both felt that it was the right step for her. She was offered a place at Trinity College, Bristol, but we knew I was going to need a job, too, so when I saw a job advertised for a Youth and Children's Worker nearby, I applied. It was a tense interview: the Easton area of Bristol is pretty tough, and as five of us sat waiting we could hear some commotion going on outside. I couldn't see the point of sitting around being nervous; after all, we were all Christians together. So I said, "Why don't we all pray that God will take charge this afternoon, and the person he wants in this job will get it." So when they came to call the first one in for the interview we were all praying together! I was quite at peace about whether I got the job or not, according to God's will, and I got it! It was very reassuring to know that God's plan included work for both of us in Bristol.

We left the Southampton outreach work in good heart: my replacement, Erica, was a very efficient person, and she was supported by a team of dedicated volunteers. Enough money had been raised for a superb new custom-built bus, and I knew the project would go from strength to strength.

We moved to Bristol and into St Jude's vicarage: the garden was overrun with rats, but we had cats, so everyone was happy and the cats had a field day! I was working alongside the vicar and a staff team, and Gillian started her course at college. In her second term Gillian discovered she was pregnant – we were pleased, but it was a bit of a shock for the college. She managed to keep attending lectures and writing her assignments right up to the end of the summer term in the first year; although she got very tired, she was determined not to miss out on any part of the course. We were overjoyed when little Leah was born – a beautiful baby with lots of dark hair – in October. Gillian went back for the second year of her course taking Leah with her, studying with her books on top of the table and one foot rocking the baby underneath. Somehow she managed to combine the baby-care with writing her essays, and she did remarkably well. By the end of the course Leah was nine months old, and crawling around, which made life in college livelier than ever! I was so proud of her – not just because she was our precious baby, but because at last I had my very own family.

Meanwhile I had learned my way around the new parish. I loved the Easton area with its mix of different ethnic groups, black, Indian, Asian and Chinese; the shops selling food from all over the world, and the different languages spoken in every street. At the same time there was a great deal of unemployment and poverty in the area, with all the problems of deprivation and crime that can come along with them. We had our share of lost and lonely people, broken families, a hostel for the homeless, and of course some young people who were bored and looking for excitement through drink or drugs or crime. I always felt specially concerned for them, because I saw the risk of my own drift into despair being repeated in their lives.

I was also aware that my own emotional problems had not gone away, and there was still work for God to do in healing me. I was having trouble sleeping, and suffering from panic attacks, so the doctor referred me to the local hospital. There I was diagnosed with Post-Traumatic Stress Disorder – the sort of condition you associate with people who have survived a serious accident, or soldiers after a battle. I was distressed to realise that I was still suffering from the after-effects of my traumatic experiences, but it wasn't surprising. For a long time when I first became a Christian, I was looked after with loving concern by communities of Christians in the Ichthus Christian Fellowship and Lee Abbey, and supportive couples like Tony and Sylvia, Joey and Bridie, and Julie and Ian. Now I wasn't on the receiving end of so much help, but was offering help to others in my turn – giving out more than taking in. It was satisfying, but my own needs hadn't entirely gone away, even with the love and support of my own family.

Fortunately I was working with a great church, where the congregation and the staff were full of enthusiasm for the gospel, but they, too, were under a great deal of pressure in the tough area in which we lived and worked. They couldn't be expected to give me as much support as I was used to. They wanted to tell people about the Saviour who could change their lives, and bring them into a new relationship of love with God. We prayed together regularly for all the problems around us, and as lives were changed we found that reaching out with the gospel was very exciting.

Home life in the vicarage was a bit too exciting, though. It wasn't a quiet street: homeless youngsters set our wheely bin on fire when they wanted to warm themselves up and have a drinking party. They used to urinate over the wall; sometimes they tried to break into the vicarage, or smash the car up. That was everyday life. Several times I was attacked at the door of the vicarage, when someone knocked on the door to ask for a sandwich and then attacked me for no reason. One morning I opened the front door and a guy went for my throat. I struggled free and managed to push him outside and slam the door shut while Gillian phoned for the police. Our vicar was sympathetic: he'd been burgled lots of times and had his car burnt out, too, yet he stayed faithfully at his post in this difficult area.

It wasn't all bad. I found it easy to relate to the young people I met on the streets, because I'd been there myself. They were usually honest with me – if they didn't want to know about God, they said so, but some of them genuinely wanted help to change their lifestyles. Once we arranged for a band to come and play at the church and invited all the young people we'd contacted. Hardly anyone turned up, and I was really disappointed. Still, I knew it didn't matter if there were only a few; if even one of them came to know God's love, it was worth any amount of effort. I remembered the times in my own life when various events had planted the seeds of understanding about God: it had been a long time before they came to life. We were planting seeds here, and whether I was there when they came to life was not for me to worry about. We had a youth group of around 30 youngsters, and many of them came to know God through the group, which was encouraging. Meanwhile there were problems to deal with every day.

One day I was coming home in the car when I found a van parked behind the vicarage. I stopped in front of it and watched: young men were coming out of the church carrying the drums, the sound equipment and all sorts of things. I went up and said, "Can I help you, lads?" I was wearing a short-sleeved tee shirt showing all my tattoos, so they thought I was one of the lads. They said, "Yeah, give us a hand will yer?" Then I said, "Hang on, this is my church, I work here." They were a bit shaken, but they started saying that they weren't really stealing; all these things just happened to be lying around. I told them I was a Christian, and that the stuff they had taken belonged to the church: it was God's church and God's stuff. "My car's going to stay right here so you can't drive off," I said quietly. "You'll find it a bit heavy carrying the drum kit and everything down the road." They all looked gobsmacked, so I asked them to help me put all the equipment back in the church. They answered with a few choice words and ran off; their Dad was waiting for them outside the pub down the road. Eventually I carried all the stuff back into the church myself, called the police, gave them a statement and finally sat down for a time of prayer. In spite of the fact that the boys had run off without any trouble, I felt a bit shaken. I'd been praying for God's protection all the time – there could easily have been a big fight, and I didn't want to be stabbed or beaten. I'd had enough of that in my young days, and I had a family now.

The following week as I was working in the Youth Club, I heard a commotion outside and went out to investigate the noises. To my horror a boy of about thirteen was firing an air gun indiscriminately at the passing traffic. I crept up behind him and distracted him by putting one hand on his shoulder – with the other I took the gun from him and fired the remaining ammunition into the ground. The police arrived and manhandled him onto the ground, bundled him into the car and drove off. When they returned later to interview me about the incident, I admitted that I'd been scared, but told them I knew God was protecting me. They just grinned at one another – they were beginning to know me.

I enjoyed my job, and I knew I had the gifts to work with young people, but I started to look around for a qualification in Youth Work. I applied for a place on a course in Youth and Community Work at Bristol South and West College. I was horrified when I realised how much it would cost – about £3,000 – but we prayed that we'd find the money somehow. The youth work in our parish was done in co-operation with lots of secular agencies, and they supported our efforts in the local community. When we told them that we needed money for training, they agreed to contribute to my funding. Miraculously, all the money came in and I was able to study full-time for the Higher Diploma.

It was tough going. The course was both theoretical and practical: we had to understand about young people's development, about the way people behaved in groups, the way society was organised, and about all the agencies that might be involved in any kind of youth work. In addition we went out and worked among young people, supervised and observed by our tutors – they watched me in action in the Easton area. I always did OK in the practical work, because I had plenty of experience, but I wasn't used to writing essays. One day I was so frustrated that I threw a whole essay in the fire – and then watched in horror as it burnt away and I realised I'd have to start it all over again!

The day I received my diploma was fantastic: I was so proud. I had tears in my eyes as I realised that I – just John Robinson, brought up in care and knocked about on the streets – had achieved something special. With God's help.

When Gillian's course finished we were ready to move on again, and the Bishop announced that he had just the position in mind for us: he could use my talents for youth work and Gillian's gifts for ministry in the same parish, and we could both work part-time, to share the child care. When we visited St Winifred's, Totton, we knew that it was the right place for us.

Going back to the Southampton area was like going home, though Briardene Court was the poshest place I'd ever lived in! The houses were beautiful and the street was quiet. I knew we wouldn't be staying there for ever, but we enjoyed it while we were there. So we moved in, all three of us and the cat, and started our new life. One thing that gave me tremendous pleasure was that when I moved back into the area I was asked to return to Coxlease School in Lyndhurst, the special school I'd worked in before, but this time as a Christian counsellor. Gillian worked in the church, and I got out on the streets again, meeting young people, doing school visits, and setting up a new Streetwise project, on the same lines as the first one.

I had opportunities to speak about Streetwise at churches of several different denominations; I didn't go as an Anglican, but as a fellow Christian, telling my own story of the difference Jesus had made in my life. I sometimes got emotional about that, but it drew us together in this desperately needed work. We met together to pray for money and volunteers, and both began to arrive. Streetwise in Totton was born.

Straight away God provided me with a reliable Christian who shared the vision: James Green, a fireman, was fantastic with young people, and good for me as a support and friend. Once again the local papers covered what we were doing, and these articles led to speaking engagements with various organisations and even the local council. They were impressed that our work wasn't done by just one church, but by Christians working together, and also by the fact that I had proper youth and community work qualifications – this gave it some authority in their eyes, and so they felt able to support us by paying for the road tax, fuel, food and drink and so on.

All our work was underpinned by prayer, and I had friends who prayed with me at length over every aspect of the work. God honoured those prayers and the work went from strength to strength, both in its support from the churches and its impact on young people.

One special initiative was the transformation of the church tower. I climbed up there one day and had a good look round – it was a huge space, but crammed full of old chairs, jumble-sale stuff and pigeon muck. There were so many old hymn books I think the church mice must have been holding services up there! It was in a terrible state, but I could see that it had potential. I asked the vicar, Paul Bayes, if we could turn it into a bar or a club, and he said, "Why not? Let's go for it!" He agreed with me that it was no good getting out on the streets to meet the young people and then leaving them there. We needed something to draw them closer to the church, and the Tower was just the thing.

We had a volunteer who was a joiner, and he looked at my drawings and helped us work out what we needed; then we found electricians, plasterers and decorators who all shared our vision for the place, and they all worked for free, so we only had to pay for the materials. It took several months' hard work, but we transformed the place into a bar and youth club, with a small office for my work. The kids chose the purple paint, and friends donated the sound system and items to stock the non-alcoholic bar. The opening was fantastic, with about 200 visitors – police officers, head teachers and councillors as well as the kids – enjoying the band. It was loud, but I guess it stopped the church mice singing!

Now we had a place for the young people to go on a Saturday night. When we went out in the bus we could offer them a place to sit and chat while we were parked there, but now we had somewhere permanent. The bar was open every Saturday night for non-alcoholic cocktails, videos and music, and we usually had about 30 youngsters there. I trained up the young people to run the bar so they could own it themselves, and they loved staffing the place. It had all the standard drop-in centre advice on hand, but because it looked and felt like a bar, they didn't feel embarrassed about coming. On Sundays we ran a youth Alpha Course – an introduction to Christianity – in the Tower.

In 1998 our second daughter Natalie was born, so we were juggling two children and two jobs between us. Life was certainly complicated. Any marriage takes work, and it can be tempting to lose yourselves in busyness to avoid tackling things. Gillian's work as a curate involved long hours which couldn't be avoided, and we sometimes found it difficult to make time for each other. Added to all that was the pressure of the goldfish-bowl life in parish and community work – we sometimes felt as though our lives were being observed all the time, and that people expected us to be perfect.

Our marriage was based on our love and mutual

faith, and that helped a lot, but sometimes we wondered if it was enough. Some of the time we were trying to struggle with the still-lurking problems of my past, as well as the challenges of the present. For instance, if we ever had a row, I always felt as if it was the end, and I was in danger of losing everything all over again. Gillian could always get on the phone and have a moan to her Mum or Dad, but I had nowhere else to turn. Occasional arguments are probably healthy in a marriage – but for me they felt like a very dangerous place indeed. I knew that God was guiding my life now, but I still always felt that there was a danger that I might go back to having nothing.

To survive that sort of pressure, a marriage needs a good support network, and fortunately Gillian's family was there to provide it. When we married, they took me on too, and made a special effort to support me as well as Gillian. If we do have a row, Gillian's Mum will listen to me, too, and acts as mediator, having little chats with both of us over the phone. Her sisters are supportive, too, and her Dad is good at taking me aside for a fatherly chat over a pint. "I don't want t' tek sides, lad," he says, in his terrible joke Northern accent, and makes me laugh. They always make a special effort at birthdays and Christmas, too, because they know I don't have anyone else.

As I never had any role models when growing up, I've had to learn about family life as I go along, and Gillian's family's acceptance of me has brought me more healing than they can imagine.

Even though I was busy, I managed to take on

other tasks as well. I was surprised and pleased to be asked to be a school governor, and I was happy to do the extra work. It took up a bit of time, going to meetings and reading paperwork, but I knew I could bring a Christian perspective to the job, and it gave me further contact with the kids and with the local community. Sometimes I had meetings with the police, probation officers and social workers, who all wanted to know what we were doing and why we were doing it, and often wanted to help. The kids who came into contact with them started telling them about the times we'd got involved with them and their friends. Sometimes just pulling up in the bus was enough to stop a fight, and as one policeman said to me, "We can see that it works."

There were times when we were offered wonderful opportunities. A group of boys came up to the Tower and hung around for a while, listening to the music, before one of them plucked up the courage to tell us what they wanted. "Our mate's in hospital," he said. "He's got meningitis and they think he might die. Will you pray for him?" We sat with them as they begged God to heal their friend, and in the end he pulled through. After those prayer meetings several of them became Christians. Not every story had a happy ending, though: lots of our kids went on getting into trouble, and sometimes I went to court with them and visited them in prison. I always felt as if I should have done more for them, but I knew God was saying, "You haven't failed here. You've sown the seed. Now it's up to me, not you."

The bus and the Tower were reaching out to

young people who wouldn't usually go into a church youth club or a church building. One place where they did feel at home was at Soul Survivor – a Christian festival designed to help young people get connected with God in styles of worship that make sense to them. For quite a few years I took a group each summer to camp there for a week and to enjoy the music, the worship and the teaching. The first time they heard people speaking in tongues they wondered where they'd landed up – they thought everyone had gone mad! Once they understood that it was a special gift of the Holy Spirit they listened to the testimonies and the message of God's love with renewed interest.

We were beginning to wonder whether it was time for us to move on again, when I saw a job advertised: chaplain in a Young Offenders Institute in Market Drayton. I'd always wanted to work in a prison, since my own terrible experiences there, and I applied and was interviewed. As I left the interview room I overheard the current chaplain exclaim, "Yes! He's just what we're looking for!" That gave me a tremendous boost to my self-confidence, and I felt I was really being valued for myself, if the Home Office would accept someone with my record to do that work. When we received a formal offer, Gillian started looking for a job nearby, but then we were devastated to get a letter from the Prison Governor revoking the offer, and saying that he wasn't happy for me to be appointed. I was furious that we had nearly given up our current jobs, and wrote to the current Home Secretary, Jack Straw, complaining about the way we were treated. He must have spoken to someone, because shortly afterwards the original offer was renewed.

By this time I was thoroughly confused: was this job part of God's will for us or not? I'd felt high when I got an offer that seemed to value me, and low when it seemed that my past was always going to be a mill-stone round my neck. I didn't know what to think.

Then I met Andy Hawthorne at Soul Survivor, and asked if he would bring The Tribe to play in Southampton. He agreed to chat with them about it, but he wanted to ask me something in return. He said that God had told him that I was just the person they needed to head up their bus ministry in Manchester – would I think about it?

I would certainly think about it. Whenever we told people that both Gillian and I had a vocation to work for God, they'd say that it was impossible for us to get two jobs in the same place. We'd always have to make one person's job a priority. However, we trusted God to find our work for us, and just as Andy was making me that offer, the Bishop of Bolton was offering Gillian a choice of two jobs in the Manchester Diocese. She accepted one of the posts, and we set about handing over the reins of the work in Southampton to James Green and the rest of the team to take it forward.

Chapter **9**

# THE BUS
# MINISTRY

LEAVING SOUTHAMPTON WAS HARD: we'd made so
many good friends, and there were so many young
people I'd got to know and love. I knew I had to trust
the rest of the team to go on guiding and nurturing
those young Christians. There were lots of good
things about the move, though. Gillian's new parish
was in a beautiful old mill town, set amid the lovely
scenery of the Pennines. The vicarage had wonderful
views out across the hills and dales, and there was an
added bonus for me: the people understood my
accent when I said "Hello love!" in my cheery way. I
felt at home straight away. I was excited and nervous
at the same time.

The Message started in 1988 as a one-week event
designed to reach out with the message of Jesus to
young people in the Manchester area. Since then it
has grown and developed; the original music and
dance group, "The World Wide Message Tribe" are
now known as The Tribe. The individual members of
The Tribe are fantastic Christians and very talented
people who work hard for God, and I'm very fond of
them. They play all over the country, but their vision
is for Manchester, and they choose to spend most of
their time there. The organisation as a whole is

involved in a range of activities designed to reach young people: high-energy youth events, counselling and advice, city-wide outreach, sports and creative arts clubs in schools, and of course the Eden bus ministry which I manage.

The Eden buses are like mobile youth centres, reaching out to exactly the kind of kids I care most about – the lost, deprived ones, drifting into drink, drugs and crime because they can't see anything else to do. Nowadays they're called "socially excluded". But the buses are a good resource for all the young people in these deprived areas of Manchester, not just those who may get into trouble – they're a good place if you just want to chill out with your mates. The Eden teams themselves are wonderful people who live and work in the inner-city areas. They do amazing work, and choose to live in deprived and often volatile areas where drug and alcohol abuse, fighting, crime and all sorts of social problems abound. I was amazed at the commitment of these Christians; they weren't just waffling about the gospel, but living it out in a way that was remarkable. To be a Christian witness in such circumstances takes some guts. You have to put up with verbal abuse, burglaries and vandalism. When I saw all this I knew I wanted to work with them for God.

The bus was magnificent: a businessman had given around a quarter of a million pounds to pay for a big double decker and fit it out. I was asked to manage the project and we set about equipping it with a big wide screen upstairs for the schools and evening work. A drinks machine, video and a top-of-the-range sound system were also installed, together with DVDs and games consoles, and we had security cameras and an office as well as places for counselling or just relaxing chats.

My first challenge was to swallow my pride. I thought I was going to manage the project, but I found I also had to learn to drive the bus. I didn't want to think of myself – much less be introduced – as a bus driver! It became another work of God in my life, to show me that I'm no less important to him whether I'm driving the bus, cleaning it or talking about it. On the first day I stood beside it and thought, "How on earth does it turn a corner?" It was 40 feet long and eight feet wide, and the very idea of driving this monster frightened the pants off me! I thought, "I'd rather be evangelising in the Bahamas than doing this!" It took a bit of time to get used to driving it; one day my instructor said, "Why don't we stop at McDonald's?" I thought, "You're off your trolley, mate. How do we get this thing into McDonald's?" Then I realised – it wasn't a drive-through! We just went into the car park and parked up, went in and bought a meal and took it back to the bus. Inside, I put some music on: I chose "Jumping in the house of God" much to the instructor's amusement.

Eventually I passed the test, and started off going round Manchester in the bus, finding the places where young people hung around, and linking with the existing Eden teams in those areas. I also drove to Spring Harvest at Minehead: handling this big bus in the winding Devon lanes was scary, but it gave me the experience I needed and the confidence that I could handle it. The roads in Devon are full of holidaymakers in their cars, sucking humbugs, looking out of the window, and shouting at the children. I confess I'd never prayed so hard in my life for safety on the road! Once we arrived we had thousands of people of all ages coming to look inside the bus. We had opportunities to talk about the work of the Eden Teams and tell them about the message of good news that we were spreading. I felt very privileged to be part of it all.

I was really glad to be part of the ministry team, and I think I fitted in easily. There was just one occasion when I gave them a bit of a shock. I was sitting chatting with Andy Hawthorne, and as it was a hot summer day, I'd rolled up my tee-shirt sleeves. I couldn't understand why Andy was staring at my right arm with a horrified expression on his face. These days I'd half forgotten all the old tattoos. Andy said very politely, "Would it be possible, John, for you to have that young lady's upper half covered up?" He was referring to a naked lady tattooed on my arm! I laughed and said, "No, don't be daft," and offered to lay hands on him to pray against the spirit of lust! Then I realised that he was being quite serious. I felt a bit angry, because if God accepted me and had cleansed me from all the past, I felt other people should be able to do the same. God set me free from all those feelings of inferiority, and from my fear of not fitting in. However, I gave the matter some serious thought and realised that it could cause offence, so I suggested to Andy that I could have a nice bra tattooed on the lady friend of the past! Maybe it could be done on expenses – we liked the thought of the accountant reading the spreadsheet and seeing "bra tattooed on John's naked lady – £20.00" !

When we got home to Manchester after Spring Harvest I settled into the routine of the bus ministry. Often we go and do school classes during the day, and in the evenings, each bus visits an area where the Eden teams are based. In addition to this, we work on our own in one tough area where the police pay us to go – they recognise that the work makes a difference in the lives of needy youngsters, including the crime rate! We also support churches throughout Manchester with outreach events they organise. In the evenings there might be between 50 and 100 youngsters coming onto the bus to have a drink, play computer games, and talk to the voluntary workers who chat and play with them. Before we set out we always spend time in prayer. Those evening prayer times are the backbone of the Eden bus ministry; we need the confidence and protection that comes from trusting God. Some of the young people we work with are affected by violence, drugs, alcohol and abuse. I'm always thankful that kids are willing to come inside, and that we can help them see another way of living.

At the end of the evening we have a session called the "God Zone", fifteen minutes before we close. We shut down all the other activities, and tell the kids about other events like the cell groups and Planet Life (where we have guest speakers like the Olympic medallist Jonathan Edwards and our own Andy Hawthorne, and Christian bands play music with a gospel message). Then we have a presentation – a testimony, video or drama – and close with prayer. The number of young people who make a commitment at this time is astounding.

Team work on board the bus is vital. My colleague Wayne Penfold is a lovely guy, quiet and unassuming but as steady as a rock. He has ten years' experience in working with young people, and they always take to him. We've been in some sticky situations together, when guns and knives have been flashed, and I'd trust him with my life on the streets. We also depend on our Accelerate workers, young people who come and join us for five months or so at a time and then move on. They give endless hours of their time, and they're a fantastic, energetic resource for the bus ministry, which couldn't operate without them. They're young and dynamic, they haven't been jaded by church politics or habit, and their instinctive, fresh response to the young people they meet gives everyone a lift. Also, without the Eden Bus team drivers (and their families) who willingly give of their time, we would not have a bus ministry at all.

We've never had any vandalism inside the bus, and I put that down to prayer, team work, and the professionalism of the staff. All our volunteers have been police checked, and I train them all in handling aggression. I'm very strict about people feeling good about the work: if anyone's tired or upset, or had a bad day, I encourage them to go home.

In balance with all the bus ministry I also have my family life, and that's very important to me. Gillian's job is supposed to be part-time, but like any work involving people, it doesn't always keep strict hours. We're both under pressure to be constantly available to others. We have to juggle the demands of our work, find time for each other, and give time to our children and nurture their faith, too. When Gillian first arrived her church was very small, with only about 20 active members. God has done amazing things there, and she now has a wonderful church family who are walking with God together. I help with the youth work and run a Men's Breakfast, as well as doing my regular "vicar's wife" bit! We manage to have one day off a week together, because we aren't able to share our evenings (when I'm not out with the bus, Gillian is dealing with church events and meetings). Our emphasis is on arranging our priorities so that we can support each other, and on the whole we make it work successfully. It's great to see both ministries developing side by side.

The bus was involved in Message 2000, a big youth event in Heaton Park, when thousands of young people came and listened to bands like Delirious, The Tribe and Why. We took the bus out every day. One evening when I was driving, a man came out of the pub and saw us. He must have had a few too many, and shouted, "Hang on! it's me bus!" Our bus isn't easy to miss: it has "The Message" emblazoned on the side, and pictures of the band everywhere – it certainly doesn't look like a number nine! I leaned out and said, "Sorry, mate, it's not a service bus," but he wasn't very happy and demanded to come on board. The young volunteers thought it was very funny.

Another day we made news on TV when the bus

developed gearbox trouble and we were stranded on the central reservation of the M62. The police were understanding when we explained that we'd got a mechanical problem, but they were fascinated by the interior of the bus and wanted a guided tour! We put the generators on and made a cup of tea, and answered their questions about our work and what powered us. Eventually the breakdown service arrived and we got the bus safely back to the depot, but it was a great opportunity to tell yet more people what Message 2000 was all about.

In fact our relationship with the police has always been good – they can recognise when people are trying to make things better, and respect our teams for going into areas of the city most people avoid. One evening the bus was in one of the usual volatile areas, parked on the site of a disused factory. Around 40 or 50 young people came along to talk, and as usual some had had too much to drink or were on drugs. As this particular evening wore on, we tried to stop the youngsters who were very drunk from coming inside the bus. They didn't like it and started smashing bottles and threatening the volunteers. The situation was turning nasty and we wondered if we'd have to call the police – we didn't want to, because "grassing" to the police is a sure way of ruining any relationship we might have been able to build up. We did manage to calm them down eventually, and drove off. Further down the road we stopped and prayed together for protection for ourselves and for the safety of those kids, and that some of them would come back and ask about God.

The following week we went back to the same place and the same crowd turned up. This time there were no problems, and some of them even apologised and asked me how I'd ended up doing this weird job. To our amazement they joined in with the prayer at the end of our meeting. Two of the girls who were the ringleaders are now regularly attending an Eden Team cell group, where they're working through their problems. The team are praying that they'll eventually give their lives to God.

Some of the youngsters we meet have really awful home backgrounds – and if *I* say they were awful you can guess they must have been bad. One night a little girl of eight or nine was hanging round the bus, but I wouldn't let her on board because she was too young – we had a few big lads inside who'd had a lot to drink. I got off the bus to talk to her; she was wrapped up in a big black coat, several sizes too large. I was trying to make her laugh, so I did a handstand, and said, "Now you do one."

"I can't," she said. "My coat'll slip off and I've got no clothes on."

Her Mum had sold her clothes to get money for drugs, and she'd stolen her Mum's coat so she could get out of the house. I wanted so much to give her a hug, and to go out and buy her some clothes, but I couldn't do either. I could only pray for her. Another night we picked up a nine-year-old girl who through the evening with her friends had drunk three-quarters of a bottle of vodka. When she collapsed her friends ran off and left her. We took her home, and afterwards she came back to see us and talked about how she could change her life. It broke my heart to hear a child as young as that say that her life was horrible and she wanted to change it.

One evening we parked the bus outside one of the local Christian centres. That area is all multi-storey blocks of flats, which seem to come alive when the bus arrives. Dozens of kids appear; some come inside the bus and others stand around it talking and sometimes fighting. On this night some of the kids started removing the windscreen wipers, and some were trying to get into the generator room. We could see some of the others in the street nearby, busy removing slates from house roofs and vandalising a street light! We were praying that God would calm the situation down, but eventually we thought we'd better pull the bus out as things were getting too volatile. Then, just as we started the engine, two of the worst troublemakers came up to the door. We were gobsmacked when they said, "What's all this Jesus stuff about, then, mate?" These two are now linked into the local Eden Team and are growing in their faith.

One 16-year-old told me she was scared about what would happen when she went to court – she'd been charged with wounding and kidnapping. Wayne and I sat and listened to her sincerely praying for forgiveness for what she'd done, and asking God to help her if she got a custodial sentence. Then she started praying for the team on the bus. She did end up in jail and we visited her there. Just before her release she wrote me this letter.

Dear John

Hi :) hope everything is OK at home, hope the EDEN team are all OK. I come home soon, I can't wait! I go to church every weekend to pray for everyone so you better had be ok 'cos God told me you was. Did you have a good Christmas? My Christmas was ok but it was just another day to me. Everyone was upset but I've learned to control myself now. I'm always thinking about everyone but there is no point in crying anymore. I just look at people who are in here for years and really i'm very lucky.

I'm now 10 weeks pregnant and it's killing me. I keep being sick and I can't sleep that well. It's horrible in here, my Christmas dinner was a thin slice of turkey, some mash potato and three roast potatoes. It's a shame but that's what everyone gets but with veg. I've been writing some things about what it's like in here to try and stop kids from getting into trouble before it's too late. I've sent them with this letter so if you get the chance too please read it to them because I don't want them to end up like me... I don't want to upset anyone I just want them to know what reality is. I'm 17 and even I cant cope, these kids are getting into trouble at the age of 12 and I really don't want them to be in a place like this, you lose all your confidence and everyone needs that. What child would want to show their body to complete strangers, but you have no choice, some people don't come out alive.

I really want to do something to help stop

people getting into trouble before it's too late. I'm going to ask when I get out if I can go into schools and talk to them so at least they have a chance in life. Nobody listens to their family – I never did, so hopefully they will listen to someone who is a kid just like them. Please help me John. I see people in here and it really worries me for the people who will end up like this. Thank you all for praying for me... most of all I cant wait to see my family, wow, its like a dream seeing my little brothers smiling. I've missed out on a lot with them. I will make it up to them when I get out and that I can promise. I'm going to spoil them rotten! I'm always dreaming about picking them up at 3.30 from school and seeing the look on their faces, after not seeing them for 2 months.

... One of the girls in here keeps crying because I go home soon but I cant wait, I've done my time. People like me because in here. There are some people who you cant trust but if I have got what they need I will give it to them and try my best to help people who are upset. If someone asks me a question I won't lie to them just to make them feel better, I will tell the truth...

Anyway, I hope people are taking care of your bus and not causing you trouble as usual. You know it makes me wonder now I'm not there for people to point the finger at who gets the blame now. No actually, I bet they still blame me saying "Well she might be in Yorkshire but it was still her who smashed that window." You know it makes me laugh looking back. People had nothing better to do than blame me for something I didn't do. I really hate it in here but sometimes I would rather be in here than at home getting the blame for everything and that is bad! I better go now cos I'll be boring you if I carry on. Take care and I will see you soon, oh, and happy new year.

Lots of love
Sara.

When you get enough of these changes among young people, and they have a change of heart and of lifestyle, it makes a noticeable difference to what goes on in an area. Some of the worst estates have actually experienced a drop in crime, as the gangs split up and some of their leaders stop causing trouble. The bus work has been so successful in this area that it has been recommended for a police award. Reducing crime isn't our primary aim, but it's good to see it as a side-effect of reaching young people for Christ. Another letter, from Sergeant Bob Pell, gives an idea of the police view of our work.

Dear John,
I am writing to you as I feel that after twelve months of working in partnership in the Weaste area of Salford I would like to take stock of the work we have been doing and review its progress.
As you are aware our paths crossed during Operation Weaste and Seedley, the five-day event that took place under the auspices of Greater Manchester Police's "Make a Difference" scheme

in August 2001. This involved a large number of agencies coming together with the common goal of working with the local community to perform gardening tasks, clear up derelict areas and to refurbish two sites that could be used as a community resource in the long term.

The Operation was very successful and attracted a lot of interest from the media, as well as the Home Office, who having witnessed the results are seriously looking at ways of selling this idea to all areas of the country.

The Eden bus project was instrumental in the overall success of the event as it attracted a large number of youths in the area and engaged them in positive activities. Whenever the Eden bus was there the number of reported incidents reduced dramatically in that location and it was that fact that drew my attention most. I was very concerned that once the event had concluded I had nothing in place to offer the same youths who had been very problematic prior to the event. I was therefore delighted that you agreed to offer the support of your team for a twelve-month period in the Weaste area primarily to engage with youths varying from eight to fourteen years who had no real facilities and no one trying to engage them in something meaningful.

Since your involvement, albeit once a week, we have been able to do just that and the feedback from the youths concerned and their parents has been very positive indeed. One or two youths are still problematic and are a cause for concern, but given the level of social deprivation and associated social problems being experienced in the area, this was only to be expected. But John, this was our challenge and remains so. I will not give up.

… The local youths still flock to you and your team each week which speaks volumes. The number of reported incidents whilst you are there still reduces significantly which highlights how well your team engages the youths.

… The reason the project has triumphed is directly down to the dedication, patience, understanding and leadership you have displayed throughout which I know not only inspires your team members, but also gives youths the confidence to return each week. It is not only my intention to continue the partnership (subject to funding, which I know is not your main consideration) in the Weaste area, but I would now like to explore the possibility of expanding your involvement into the Irlams o' th' Height, which is also experiencing similar problems.

John, to summarise, I believe you and your team are contributing to the long-term solution in Weaste and will continue to do so. I would recommend that any organisation who has a duty to improve the quality of people's lives as well as work directly with youth to consider a different approach than normally taken and work with the Eden Bus project. I am delighted I did and look forward to a long and successful partnership.

Yours sincerely
Police Sergeant Bob Pell
Pendleton Police Station
Salford.

Not all the young people who come on the bus take drugs or drink too much. Lots of them are just ordinary youngsters, and God works in their lives too. Not every changed life is a dramatic change to the outside eye, but it is just as important.

Not long ago the original donors who gave us the money for the first bus came along to see it in action. They were so impressed that they've given us the funding for a second vehicle: they want to see our ministry doubled. This means more staff and more volunteers, and it's great to see both coming forward to support us. I believe the bus ministry has a great future in Manchester, reaching young people with down-to-earth acceptance and love, and sharing the gospel with them.

Chapter 10

# PASSION FOR THE GOSPEL

WE WERE SETTLED IN MANCHESTER, and both our jobs were going well and giving us a lot of satisfaction. God was working in amazing ways in Gillian's church and in the bus ministry. The girls were settled in the local primary school, just a few minutes' walk from our front door, and growing up to be beautiful, mischievous children. Life was good: just as I'd always dreamed, I now had a family of my own. We've celebrated ten years of marriage and I adore my two girls. So had we arrived in happy-ever-after land? The answer is no. Nothing's ever quite that easy. Although I'd turned my back on the misery of my early life, it hadn't entirely left me.

Healing isn't necessarily instantaneous; it takes time. I accepted Jesus into my life in a moment, but working out how to follow him goes on every day of my life. Just as my change of attitude took time – all those years in London, the Isle of Wight and at Lee Abbey, where I was learning to take responsibility for my actions, and how to handle my relationships with other people – so it was taking time for my mind and body to be healed.

When we become Christians, God doesn't promise to protect us from every evil – only that he'll be alongside us to love and support us. He doesn't say that we'll never have any troubles in our life, only that we won't be defeated by them. I still had some battles to fight and some weaknesses to acknowledge. This can be hard if people want to turn you into some kind of a figurehead: the man whose life was transformed by God. It's true: I can put my hand on my heart and say that if God hadn't intervened in my life I'm pretty sure that I wouldn't be here today. I'd have died on the streets through illness or violence or just giving up in despair. I'll never forget a psychiatrist saying to me that he was at a loss how to help me: he'd never met anyone who'd suffered my level of rejection and abuse who hadn't committed suicide! But even though God saved me from all that, I know I still bear the scars of that time, not only on my skin but in my heart.

Sometimes the signs are funny. It's a standing joke in our family that whenever we pack to go away on holiday, even for a weekend, I'll have a couple of huge suitcases. I always over-pack. Other men joke about their wives taking too much stuff with them; Gillian laughs at me. It's partly related to those days when I was little and "collected things like a magpie" – when you haven't got much to call your own, every tiny thing becomes important, and you're unwilling to let go of anything. Partly it's related to the later times when I had no home and no settled base, and I had to carry everything around with me in a broken-down old rucksack or a black bin-liner. If I left anything behind, it wouldn't be there when I got back. They're old habits and hard to break. I suppose it all stems from a fundamental insecurity. No one knows how great or how long-lasting the damage is when a child is fearful and insecure and unloved from his earliest days.

Other signs are more serious: for a long time I kept reliving the past in nightmares and flashbacks. Sometimes I had vivid dreams, and woke up shouting and sweating. Sometimes I had insomnia and panic attacks, tossing and turning as the hours went by, with a knot of tension in my stomach that wouldn't go away, even though I tried to relax and pray. It was as if my body was in the habit of being tensed against anything unexpected that might happen, and even now, safe in my own bed, I couldn't lose the habit.

Gillian suffered through these times with me, not only by being woken when I sat up in bed, shouting and trembling, but by seeing me upset and depressed because the problems of my past still wouldn't go away. Sometimes my nights seemed as busy and eventful as my days – but a lot less enjoyable. You can't be rational in your dreams, and going to bed at night could be a fearful experience. Would I slip into the nightmare where I was shut in a dark, cold cellar with only a thin line of light showing under the locked door? Or would it be the hot prison cell, with a foul smell and the sound of distant screams? Or would I dream that I was hunched uncomfortably in a doorway, waiting for someone to spring out at me and cut me with a flick-knife? Sometimes I started the day exhausted.

For many years I used smoking as a way of calming my nerves, even though I always felt guilty about spending money on cigarettes, and of course I knew about the health risks. Then Gillian's sister (who has never smoked) was diagnosed with cancer, and that kick-started me into doing something about it. It was a struggle, but eventually I managed to give up. Now I have enormous sympathy for people who try to give up and fail, and enormous admiration for those who succeed. I know how hard it is.

There are a lot of issues like that: when you've been there yourself, you have a much greater under-standing of what people go through. It can make you more sympathetic, and more willing to offer a help-ing hand whenever you can. For several years now I've gone on sponsored bike rides around the world to raise money for National Children's Homes – now called NCH Action for Children. This charity does a lot of work in caring for children who have been abused, or have disabilities, or need fostering or adoption. They run Family Centres where children can play and learn to relate to other people, and Mum or Dad can get help with parenting to enable them to cope with their kids – the kind of support that can mean that the children don't have to go into care. Because I was brought up in care this charity appeals to me, and I'm more than willing to give up some time and energy to support it. Actions speak louder than words, and though I may never meet the current children in care, my attempts at fund-raising are a way of putting an invisible arm around them saying, "I love you." I know from my own experience how easy it is for young people with no guidance or super-vision to drift into the wrong company, into crime and the cycles of deprivation that lead to homelessness, poverty and despair. I'm happy to help the people who can step in and try to break the pattern for these children.

One year the ride was in Thailand, and that was an eye-opener for me. I enjoyed the bustle of the street markets with all the colourful goods at cheap prices, but there was another side to life there which was equally cheap but nasty. We were told of nine- and ten-year-old girls who danced in the bars and were used as prostitutes. They'd been sold by their fathers, often as a way of paying their gambling debts. I felt both sad and angry as I saw English, German and other tourists using those places. They didn't care about the plight of the girls. It was quite scary to realise that it was an accepted part of life: the police were just walking past, and no one batted an eyelid at this horrible trade. There were other kinds of exploitation, too. I looked out of my hotel window one night and saw a little child of no more than two years old. He was filthy and covered in dust, sitting on the pavement begging for money. The parents were hiding nearby while tourists took photos. I was sickened by the heartlessness of the average tourist. It made me realise that there are children all over the world, not just in England, who need love and protection.

Here in Manchester we are doing what we can to help vulnerable young people. We know that preaching the gospel of God's love is the most important thing we can do, but we have to do it in ways that they can understand. Offering them friendship is the first step. We keep looking for ways to make the gospel message relevant to young people. It's always the same message, but there are different ways of communicating it. Some of these kids don't have any interest in going to church, but the bus ministry gives us a unique opportunity to meet young people on their own terms and on their own territory.

If I have a vision for the future, it's that we can go far beyond anyone's expectations of what such a ministry can achieve. I want the bus ministry to develop without being afraid of what other people will think, or the limits which other people impose on it, because if it's what God wants us to do, it will work. This is an area which is often hard for me, because I'm not always very self-confident, and I sometimes find it difficult to hold on to a vision when people say it won't work. Yet we have faith in God and in the young people, and if they want what we're offering, then much, much more can happen.

We have to go on building our relationships with all the other agencies, so that they can see we're not just Bible-bashing. They can help us to offer love to the kids in practical ways – food, accommodation and advice where they need it. We want to give them the opportunity to understand what God wants for them: a fulfilled, free life, in which they are loved and respected as individuals. Some of them have already got huge problems in their lives, but my own experiences have taught me never to judge a book by its cover. People have judged me by my appearance often enough, and come to the wrong conclusion. I remember once Gillian and I drove in a tremendous downpour to the church where she was curate and I worshipped. I went to see whether the church door was open, leaving Gillian to keep dry in the car. While I was gone the church organist, who hadn't been there very long, came over and spoke to her through the window.

"I think that man's trying to break in. Shall I call the police?" Gillian had to reassure him and explain that I was not at all dangerous, and was actually her husband!

All of us need to treat people with the respect they deserve – and all of us deserve to be loved. No matter what our background may be, we have the same needs and feelings, and everyone is hurt by rejection. Whatever a person's status may be, if we take away the money, the possessions and the smart clothes, underneath is a vulnerable human being who needs love and affection.

I try to meet young people where they are, whether they're on the street, or involved in drink or drugs, without judging them or making them feel bad about themselves. If we can get alongside them and accept them and offer them our support, we make it possible for them to see that they can make changes in their lives. God can meet them wherever they are, and when we are able to share the gospel with them in a relevant way, we can leave the rest of it up to God. He alone knows what is in each person's heart, and can touch them with his love.

It's important to show them that that they can move on from the past, without dwelling on it. Too often people assume that these young people growing up in deprived areas, exposed to abuse and neglect and drifting into trouble, can't ever change. I'm the living proof that it isn't true. I was once where they are – and in worse places – but God changes lives: he changed mine. The Devil tried to destroy my life with hurt and rejection, but God is powerful enough to turn all that round and use it for his glory. I burn with the urgent message for young people that there is nothing so bad that God can't turn it round and use it for good.

At the same time, I don't want to preach a sanitised, over-the-rainbow gospel. As Christians we aren't Muppets, all soft and stuffed with fluff. We have to have a hard love, that doesn't disguise the reality of everyday life. I don't want to pretend that you can become a Christian and everything will be hunky-dory, because it won't. There are no magic wands. My life has been tough, and after 16 years of being a Christian I've had to work through some hard times, and had to do battle with myself as well as with circumstances. Even now I know that some Christians find it hard to accept me – because of my appearance or the way I talk or just because of who I am – but it doesn't matter. I am secure in knowing that God accepts me, with all my rough edges, and he loves me.

I don't want to set myself up as a role model, and I don't want to spend my time pretending to be something I'm not. When I'm involved in church meetings I can get exasperated when things get bogged down in politics or issues I don't think are important. Yet when I'm working on the streets I'm full of energy and enthusiasm for what I do. I feel at peace, because I know I'm where God wants me to be. He has taken the raw material of my ordinary self – my friendliness and cheerfulness and my ability to get on with people – and turned it into gifts that he can use to do his work, reaching the kids and taking an interest in them. All those painful experiences of my early life have not been forgotten or deleted but transformed. They are the reason I am able to identify with the young people I meet, and to be accepted by them. My past has given me the ability to assess and handle the very violent and volatile places where we work in Manchester. After years of having no security or affection in my own life, I can tell people with confidence and integrity that there is someone who isn't going to let you down. God will always love you unconditionally.

My story is unusual in some ways, and yet what I've discovered over the years of being a Christian is that whatever our personal story, God cares for us and is interested in us as individuals. Since I decided to follow Jesus I have let God down many times, and yet he has never let me go. I know that his love and care is available to you, too, and that God has a plan for your life, which is fuller and more exciting than anything you could dream for yourself.

As a family, we don't know what the future will hold. We may move on in time, and when God calls I hope and trust we will listen prayerfully and obediently. We don't know what's around the corner, but right now it's good to see what's happening where we are. Our God is a great God who does wonderful things, in our lives and in the lives of those around us, and every week we have the excitement of seeing young people discovering the life-changing power of his love.

*

If you would like to contact me about becoming a Christian or if you would like to see a testimony video, please e-mail me on: edenbus@message.org.uk or write to:

John Robinson
Eden Bus Manager
PO Box 151
Manchester
M22 4YY